ASSERTIVENESS AT WORK
A practical guide to handling awkward situations

ASSERTIVENESS AT WORK

A practical guide to handling awkward situations

Ken and Kate Back

McGRAW-HILL BOOK COMPANY

London · New York · St Louis · San Francisco · Auckland · Bogotá
Guatemala · Hamburg · Lisbon · Madrid · Mexico · Montreal
New Delhi · Panama · Paris · San Juan · São Paulo
Singapore · Sydney · Tokyo · Toronto

Published by
McGRAW-HILL Book Company (UK) Limited
MAIDENHEAD · BERKSHIRE · ENGLAND

British Library Cataloguing in Publication Data
Back, Ken
  Assertiveness at work: a practical guide to handling awkward situations.
  1. Personnel management   2. Assertiveness (Psychology)   3. Psychology, Industrial
  I. Title   II. Back, Kate
  658.3′001   HF5549

  ISBN 0-07-084576-X

Library of Congress Cataloging in Publication Data
Back, Ken
  Assertiveness at work.
  1. Executive ability   2. Assertiveness (Psychology)   3. Management—Psychological aspects.
  I. Back, Kate II. Title.
  HF5500.2.B2   658.4′092   82-199

  ISBN 0-07-084576-X   AACR2

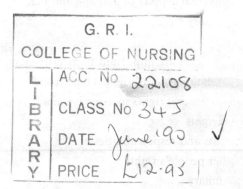
1112 AP 910

Printed in Great Britain at the Alden Press, Oxford and bound by Skyline Bookbinders Ltd

Contents

Preface   ix

1. Assertion, nonassertion and aggression   1
   - What we mean by 'assertion'   1
   - What we mean by 'nonassertion'   1
   - What we mean by 'aggression'   2
   - The effects of nonassertion   3
   - How you come to be nonassertive   6
   - The effects of aggression   9
   - How you come to be aggressive   13
   - Why be more assertive?   15
   - Some concluding considerations   18

2. Recognizing assertive, nonassertive and aggressive behaviour   21
   - Verbal aspects of behaviour   21
   - Recognition exercise: assertive, nonassertive and aggressive behaviours   25
   - Nonverbal aspects of ass, agg and n.a.   31
   - Summary   34

3. Rights!   35
   - Why rights are important to assertiveness   35
   - Where do 'general' rights come from?   36
   - Your general rights in assertiveness   38
   - Job rights   40
   - Rights and responsibilities   42
   - Other people's rights   43
   - Summary   44

4. Starting to be more assertive   45
   - Situation 1. Making requests   45
   - Situation 2. Refusing requests   47
   - Situation 3. Disagreeing and stating your views   49
   - Situation 4. Giving praise   52
   - Situation 5. Receiving praise   54
   - Conclusion   55

5. Types of assertion   56
   – Six types of assertion   56
   – When to use different assertions—general notes   62
   – How to say the types of assertion—assertively   63
   – Summary   65

6. Handling negative feelings   70
   – The way many people handle feelings   70
   – Where feelings come from   71
   – The nature of the thinking process   74
   – Handling unproductive feelings   78
   – Summary   84

7. Giving and receiving criticism about performance   85
   – Giving criticism   85
       Rights involved in criticism   86
       Some common inner dialogues   86
       Guidelines for giving criticism   86
   – Receiving criticism assertively   91
       Rights in receiving criticism   92
       Inner dialogues   92
       Hints for receiving criticism   92

8. How others influence you   94
   – What we mean by influence   94
   – How aggression from others influences you   95
   – How nonassertion from others influences you   97
   – How assertion from others influences you   99
   – How people influence you through their past behaviour   99
   – Summary   100

9. Handling aggression from others   102
   – Different levels of aggression   102
   – Overcoming barriers to responding assertively   103
   – Responding assertively to aggression from others   105
   – Coping with 'everyday put-downs'   113
   – Conclusion   116

10. Handling nonassertion from others   117
   – Different forms of nonassertion   117

     – Responding assertively to nonassertion   120

     – Summary   123

11. Resolving conflict   124

     – Types of needs   124

     – Ways of handling conflict   125

     – Guidelines for resolving conflict   128

     – Some concluding comments   132

12. Contributing assertively to meetings   133

     – Inner dialogues for contributing to meetings   134

     – Your rights as a member of a meeting   135

     – Hints for contributing assertively to meetings   136

     – Conclusion   141

13. Continuing to increase your assertiveness   142

     – Choosing the 'right' situations   142

     – Preparing for situations   143

     – Behaving assertively during these situations   143

     – Reviewing situations afterwards   146

     – Handling unexpected situations   146

     – A few final words   147

Index   148

Preface

If you have to deal with other people as part of your job, then this book is meant for you. It does not matter whether you work for a large private company, a public corporation, a medium-sized family business, or a one-man concern—just as long as your work brings you into contact with other people. So whatever your job—whether you manage a number of people or are a specialist advising and influencing others—this book will be useful to you.

It is likely that in the course of your work you will face a number of tricky situations from time to time. For instance, have you ever experienced any of the following?
- Being faced with unreasonable requests from your boss
- Feeling angry about the co-operation you are getting from another department
- Having to convey a decision that you know your staff will not like
- Wanting to disagree with a point of view that a senior manager is forcefully expressing
- Having to handle an irate customer without losing his valuable business or making promises that are difficult to keep
- Making an important presentation to a group of senior managers having had very little time to prepare

We call these situations 'tricky' because they often make you feel uncomfortable, anxious, angry, or frustrated and they can sometimes lead to open conflict. Any of these things can happen when your needs, wants, beliefs, or opinions are *different* from the needs, wants, beliefs, or opinions of the other people involved. These situations, and many like them, occur in all organizations. We believe that your success at work, and thus the success of your organization, can be affected by the way you handle these situations. We say this because *the outcome of any situation can be very different according to how it is handled.*

This book is about handling these and many other situations in a way that is mutually acceptable to all parties concerned. From our own personal experiences and from working with managers we have concluded that this usually means behaving *assertively*, as opposed to *nonassertively* or *aggressively*.

So the book focuses on the *behaviour* you can use when handling various situations. The word 'behaviour' can be used to refer to a whole range of observable activities that people engage in. But we mostly use it in a particular way—to refer to *the things you do and say* when you are communicating with other people. The book also looks at what lies behind the behaviour, not in terms of general aspects of personality, but in terms of the specific beliefs, thoughts, and feelings you may have that affect the behaviour you use. We concentrate on behaviour, beliefs, thoughts, and feelings because, as we hope to demonstrate in the book, they can be changed!

Of course, it is not easy to change these things, but it can be done. With practice you can change your beliefs, thoughts, behaviour, and even your feelings, especially if you tackle them in small steps, concentrating on one, at most two, specific aspects at a time. This brings us to say something about how to use the book. If you want to get maximum mileage out of it, then we suggest you dip into the book a chunk at a time. What we had in mind when we arranged Chapters 1–7 was that you would probably want to get to grips with the preliminary concepts and then do some practice before digging further into the concepts. Chapters 8–10 are slightly different, in that they help you not only to handle tricky situations, but in particular to handle the people whose own aggressive or nonassertive behaviour makes a situation even more difficult. In Chapters 11 and 12 we look at two applications of assertiveness. Then in Chapter 13 we give some practical suggestions on how you can continue to be more assertive after you have finished reading this book.

The book presents a third option in the area of behaviour: assertiveness. It gets you to focus on *yourself*, what *you can do*, and moves you away from being at the mercy of other people's behaviour and the adverse effects this can have on you. Not only will assertiveness help you to become more effective in your job, but it will also lead to greater personal satisfaction in your dealings with other people.

We would like to thank our friend, Liz Banfield, who patiently waded through our original (and sometimes almost illegible) manuscript to produce a first class typescript for us.

Ken and Kate Back

1. Assertion, nonassertion and aggression

The word 'assertion' appeals to us because it is a familiar word rather than a new bit of jargon. The dictionary defines it in two ways: an affirmation, a declaration, or a positive statement; insistence upon a right. Unfortunately, though, in common usage the word often refers to behaviour that *we* would call aggression. These different uses can be confusing. So let us begin this chapter by clarifying the way we use the terms 'assertion', 'nonassertion', and 'aggression' to refer to three types of behaviour. We will then examine the different effects of the three behaviours and look at how people come to behave nonassertively and aggressively, ending the chapter with some general considerations about assertiveness.

What we mean by 'assertion'

We use the word 'assertion' (or the abbreviation 'ass') to refer to behaviour that involves:
- Standing up for your own rights in such a way that you do not violate another person's rights
- Expressing your needs, wants, opinions, feelings and beliefs in direct, honest and appropriate ways

We will demonstrate this with an example. Suppose your boss asked you to complete some additional work by the end of the month. You are the best person to do the work, but your time is already fully committed to other work. An assertive response in this situation could be:
'I appreciate that you would like this work completed by the end of the month. However, I don't see that I can fit it in with our workload as it is at present.'
So assertiveness is based on the *beliefs* that in any situation:
- You have needs to be met
- The other people involved have needs to be met
- You have rights; so do others
- You have something to contribute; so do others

The aim of assertive behaviour is to satisfy the needs and wants of both parties involved in the situation.

What we mean by 'nonassertion'

We use the words 'nonassertion' (or 'n.a.') to refer to behaviour when it involves the following:

– Failing to stand up for your rights or doing so in such a way that others can easily disregard them

– Expressing your needs, wants, opinions, feelings, and beliefs in apologetic, diffident, or self-effacing ways

– Failing to express honestly your needs, wants, opinions, feelings, and beliefs

So, if we return to the previous situation, a nonassertive response could be: 'Well, I don't really have any spare time, but I suppose I could work late to fit the extra work in, er . . . I don't mind.'

Nonassertion is based upon the *beliefs* that in any situation:

– The other person's needs and wants are more important than your own

– The other person has rights, but you do not

– You have little or nothing to contribute; the other person has a great deal to contribute

The aim of nonassertion is to avoid conflict and to please others.

What we mean by 'aggression'

We use the word 'aggression' ('agg') to refer to behaviour that consists of the following:

– Standing up for your own rights, but doing so in such a way that you violate the rights of other people

– Ignoring or dismissing the needs, wants, opinions, feelings, or beliefs of others

– Expressing your own needs, wants, and opinions (which may be honest or dishonest) in inappropriate ways

An aggressive response to the example situation could be:

'What! I'm up to my eyes in work already. There's no way I can do that.'

Aggressive behaviour is based on the *belief* that:

– Your own needs, wants, and opinions are more important than other people's

– You have rights but other people do not

– You have something to contribute; others have little or nothing to contribute

The aim of aggression is to win, if necessary at the expense of others.

So these are the three basic types of behaviour that all of us can use. Below is another example illustrating the three different behaviours being used to handle the same situation.

Situation	*Taking an unsatisfactory letter back to the person who has typed it*
Assertion	'Jane, I'd like you to re-type this letter as there are several mistakes in it.'
Nonassertion	You find an excuse not to take the letter back, or you say: 'I know it's, um . . . probably my fault in . . . not writing very

2

clearly, but is there, um . . . any chance at all you could find a spare minute to um . . . just change one or two small things on this letter for me.'

Aggression 'I don't know how you've got the nerve to give me this sort of stuff for signing. It's full of mistakes.'

A WORD ABOUT 'RIGHTS'

In defining the three different types of behaviour, we have referred several times to 'rights'. We go into detail on this in Chapter 3, but for the moment let us say that a right is *something to which you are entitled*. In any situation, you will have rights; other people will have rights. Thus, in the situation above, the manager has the right to expect and receive typing of the standard agreed (assuming this *has* been agreed). He has the right to point out mistakes to the typist. The typist has the right to have these mistakes pointed out in a reasonable manner, so that she is not personally under attack or made to look small. Unless you are clear on the rights in a situation, you cannot know whether you are being assertive.

We will now examine the effects of nonassertion and aggression and then look at how these behaviours come about.

The effects of nonassertion

As we have said, when you behave nonassertively you are aiming to avoid conflict and to please others. But in pursuing this aim, your nonassertion has effects: on the outcome of the situation, on yourself, on other people, and on your organization. Let us look at each of these in turn.

EFFECTS ON THE OUTCOME OF THE SITUATION

Let us return to the first situation we described. Just to recap, your boss has asked you to complete some new work by the end of the month. You are the best person to do the work, but you have no spare time available. A nonassertive response was: 'Well, I don't really have any spare time but I suppose I could work late to fit the extra work in, er . . . I don't mind.' The outcome in this situation, as a result of that particular nonassertion, is likely to be that you would agree to take on more work than you could handle in normal working hours. We would not regard this as a satisfactory outcome because it does not meet the needs *of both parties*. True, in some instances you may get what you want. All too often, though, the other person gets what he wants. Either way, these are not outcomes that meet both sets of needs. In addition, in many situations your nonassertion will lead to *low-quality* outcomes—an impractical solution, a weak compromise, an unclear or belated decision, and so on.

3

EFFECTS ON YOU

Short-term effects
Immediately after a nonassertion like the response in the previous example, it is likely that you would experience a number of effects. We cannot say precisely what these would be because we cannot observe them, but they might be any of the following:
- A reduction in anxiety because you have avoided a potential conflict with your boss
- An escape from feelings of guilt, which would have followed from upsetting your boss by saying 'No' to him
- Feeling sorry for yourself because you are the 'poor soul who gets landed with all the work'
- A feeling of pride that you take on so much work

We refer to these effects as short-term consequences, because they follow immediately after a behaviour. These immediate consequences and other similar ones are usually pleasant for you (strangely enough, you can even enjoy feeling sorry for yourself) and thus they reinforce your nonassertion. By this, we mean *they increase the chances that you will behave nonassertively again*. Let us illustrate this with an example.

Tomorrow you know you have a difficult situation to handle when you have to tell Mike, a member of your staff, that he has not been given the regrading of his job that he was expecting. You know he is going to be annoyed and will probably start blaming you for not pushing hard enough. Thinking about this makes you feel anxious and tense. When you get into work in the morning you find that Mike has phoned in to say he is sick and will not be in today. Immediately you feel a reduction in tension ('Phew! Thank goodness I shan't have to face that today'). Because this is a pleasant experience you will look for ways to repeat it. So tomorrow when Mike is in, you find an excuse not to face up to him (perhaps you are too busy in meetings). This pattern is repeated the day after, so that you are putting off facing up to a difficult situation. Your nonassertion is being reinforced.

Reinforcement can also come from other people. For instance, colleagues may say things like: 'That's very good, you're always willing to stay late', or 'You don't mind putting yourself out', or 'You never upset anyone, you don't rock the boat'. These help to reinforce your nonassertion.

While the immediate consequences of nonassertion are pleasant, the longer-term ones can be unpleasant and undesirable for yourself, for others and for the organization you work for.

Longer-term effects
Frequent nonassertion will result in your experiencing a growing loss of self-esteem. Self-esteem is the evaluation you hold about yourself as a person.

Also, other people may reinforce your nonassertion. In addition, some organizations, either unwittingly or otherwise, encourage nonassertion, for instance through a climate that discourages questioning or trying new approaches. Let us now examine some of the other reasons for nonassertion.

FEAR OF UNPLEASANT CONSEQUENCES FROM ASSERTION

You may be afraid of what might happen if you were to behave assertively in a situation. For instance, when wanting to say 'No' to a colleague's request you may be afraid that he will cease to like you or he will become angry or upset. At other times you may be anxious about having an argument, losing your job, making changes to the status quo, facing uncertainty, and so on. We have found that fear of negative consequences is a common reason for people behaving nonassertively. Such anxiety will diminish only after you have behaved assertively and have not experienced these consequences.

PERCEIVING SITUATIONS OR OTHER PEOPLE AS THREATENING

Supposing you are unsure of your ability, say, to do your job; then you would want to avoid bringing attention to yourself and would thus try to adopt a 'low profile'. So any situation, such as a meeting, that looks to be bringing you into 'public' focus, you would see as threatening. Any person making reference to your work—maybe your manager checking whether you will meet your deadlines—you would see as threatening. This could result in your behaving nonassertively by:

– Saying little in meetings
– Failing to mention problems you are having in meeting your deadlines

FAILING TO ACCEPT YOUR ASSERTIVE RIGHTS

If you do not realize or fully accept that you have certain rights, then you will not stand up for these rights. So, for example, if you do not accept that you have the right to propose to senior management some changes to a particular work procedure, then you may complain to colleagues about it, but you will not raise it with senior managers—you will be nonassertive.

FAILING TO THINK RATIONALLY ABOUT YOURSELF

This often comes about when you frequently compare yourself unfavourably to other people. An example of this would be saying things like: 'I'll never be as good as Pete at getting my ideas across'. This may or may not be true, but it will probably lead you to put your ideas forward tentatively and to withdraw

7

them at the first sign of resistance. So then your idea stands a good chance of being rejected—which confirms your first statement about yourself! Thinking of this sort maintains your nonassertion.

CONFUSING ASSERTION AND AGGRESSION
If you are brought up in an environment where nonassertion is common, you would be likely to see any firm statement of assertion from others as aggression. Because you do not want to be seen as 'aggressive', you then bend over backwards to make sure this does not happen. You do this by being unduly deferential and apologetic. This may happen if you work for an organization that encourages certain groups of its staff to be nonassertive. The organization does this because it does not realize that another alternative to being nonassertive is to be assertive rather than aggressive.

FAILING TO DEVELOP ASSERTIVE SKILLS
If you have been encouraged from early days to behave nonassertively, then these are the behaviours that you become skilled at using. As you only use assertive behaviours in 'safe' situations, you do not become skilled at such things as stating your own point of view when it is different from other people's. Alternatively, you may have had unpleasant experiences of assertion, and this has convinced you it is dangerous, or impractical, for everyone to state his needs, wants or opinions.

The result is that your behaviour pattern will contain a lot of nonassertion. Maybe there will be occasional bursts of aggression, when the tension resulting from this nonassertion becomes too much.

EQUATING NONASSERTION WITH POLITENESS
Like most of us, you have probably been brought up to be polite and considerate to others. The mistake that many people make is to believe that in order to be polite you need to be nonassertive. So, for instance, you would keep quiet rather than disagree with someone else's opinion, or shrug off rather than accept a genuine piece of praise from a colleague; whereas it is in fact quite possible to disagree and/or accept praise in an assertive way that will not be seen as impolite or inconsiderate. It is both polite and assertive to thank people or to apologize, say, if you bump into them—it is nonassertive to apologize profusely for your own opinion or for needing someone to do some work for you.

CONFUSING NONASSERTION WITH HELPFULNESS
You may believe that when you are nonassertive you are actually being helpful to the other person. In fact, the reverse may well be true. Look at this example from social life. A friend asks you and some others whether you would prefer

tea or coffee. Each of you in reply says 'I don't mind', and so at the end of the exercise the friend is no further forward in deciding which to make! In a work context a member of staff may say he does not mind when he takes his holidays, believing that he is being helpful by giving wider options, but his response does not give you specific information to plan the future workload. Not only this, but all too often people actually *do* have preferences—they do not state them because they are trying to be helpful. Later on these preferences may come to the surface when a decision is made that does not fit in with them.

Of course, there will be times when you genuinely do not have a preference and you can make this clear by behaving assertively and saying something like 'I am happy with any of those options.' This is quite different from having preferences or doubts which you keep quiet about at the time in order to be 'helpful'.

We will now explore the other side of the picture—aggression—examining the effects of this behaviour and how it comes about.

The effects of aggression

With aggression, as we have mentioned, you are aiming to win, if necessary at the expense of others. But as you do so, what effects does aggression have—on the outcome of the particular situation, on yourself, on other people, and on the organization?

EFFECTS OF AGGRESSION ON THE OUTCOME OF THE SITUATION

We will return to an example we have used several times in the chapter. Your boss asks you to complete some additional work; you are the best person to do the work; but you have no spare time available. An aggressive response to this was 'What? I'm up to my eyes in work already. There's no way I can do that!' As a result of this particular aggression the outcome is likely to go one of two ways. Your manager may end up not having the work done by you at all—an unsatisfactory outcome because it does not appear to meet his needs. Alternatively, he may become aggressive in return, saying something like 'Well, that's your problem' and pushing the work on to you regardless. This is not a satisfactory outcome either, because it does not meet your needs. So either way the outcome is not satisfactory in meeting both sets of needs. In addition, the outcome, whichever way it goes, will be of low quality because the work will probably suffer.

In many situations your aggression will produce outcomes that do not meet both sets of needs, and that are poor quality in themselves—a hasty decision, important issues getting lost, potentially useful ideas being stifled, or solutions that create further problems.

EFFECTS OF AGGRESSION ON YOU

Short-term effects

Immediately after behaving aggressively you may feel a reduction in tension owing to the release of pent-up emotions. For instance, have you ever been aware of anger building up inside yourself and, after expressing this anger, have you said to yourself 'I feel better for having said that'?

Where the aggression is successful in achieving what you want (getting your needs met), then you may feel a sense of power over others. Both this and the reduction in tension are pleasant experiences and serve to reinforce your aggressive behaviours.

Other people praising you may also serve to reinforce your aggression. For example, they may say such things as: 'You certainly told him where to get off', or 'I liked the way you put him in his place'.

There is the same dilemma as for nonassertion. The short-term consequences are pleasant and rewarding for you, while the long-term ones may well be undesirable for yourself, for other people, and for your organization. Let us look at what these are.

Longer-term effects

One of the effects is that after a while you may experience feelings of guilt or shame. This is particularly likely to occur if you more commonly behave nonassertively, only breaking into aggression from time to time. These feelings of guilt may lead you to try to make amends to the people on the receiving end of your aggression by being unduly apologetic or by being over-helpful for a while.

Instead of feeling guilt or embarrassment about your aggression you may start blaming it on other people. When you do this you will likely be in a constant state of alert, always guarding against attack from others. For instance, you may have found yourself using considerable energy, either before or during a meeting, to protect your position or your department, saying things like 'They'll be wanting to make changes. I mustn't let them get away with that.' Doubtless by the end of the day you'll be drained of energy.

Over a period of time you may well start generalizing that people are out to get you or to get one up on you (not just the people directly affected by your aggression). This can lead you to experience deepseated hate or mistrust for large groups of people ('You've got to watch shopfloor people, they're always trying to pull a fast one'). You may even feel a rage against the human race ('Everybody wants something for nothing these days'). These strong feelings can leave you feeling isolated. Alongside this, you may find it difficult to maintain friendships; you may weaken your job prospects in an organization that does not encourage aggression; or you may suffer high blood pressure.

10

So the longer-term effect of aggression on you follows this sort of pattern:

Feeling guilt or shame   or   Blaming others
↓   ↓

Apologizing profusely   Constant state of alert
or being over-helpful   ↓

                                        Being drained of energy
                                               ↓

                                        Hate and mistrust against
                                         large groups of people
                                               ↓

                                        Isolation from human race
                                         (maybe problems with friendships,
                                         job prospects, blood pressure)

As with nonassertion, the longer-term effects on you are undesirable but, because the short-term effects may be pleasant and rewarding, the aggression continues.

EFFECTS OF AGGRESSION ON OTHERS
For a while some people may feel admiration for you. Even people on the receiving end of your aggression may say things like 'He quite rightly tore me off a strip'. The admiration is not only for your aggression but also for themselves surviving in this 'tough' environment. However, more usually the person on the end of your aggression feels angry, hurt, or humiliated, feelings that lead them to want to retaliate either openly or 'underground'. When people retaliate openly—with aggressive retorts, threats, deliberate mistakes, strikes, or go-slows—then it can be clearly seen that aggression breeds aggression.

When people go underground they may retaliate by withholding information, by making sarcastic comments behind your back, or by saying one thing to your face but doing something different. An example of the latter is people quietly making it difficult for your ideas to work out in practice. The people using underground retaliation are ones for whom open retaliation may be too risky, for example staff junior to you.

Without necessarily realizing it, some subordinates take fewer initiatives as a result of your aggression and may form the habit of referring decisions to you. This is because they are not prepared to risk your aggression if their initiative did not meet your approval or their decision was wrong.

In the longer term, other people will either become resigned to you (probably behaving nonassertively in the face of your aggression), or they will leave and get a job elsewhere.

11

Thus the effects of aggression on others is along the following pattern:

Others may   or   They may feel anger,
admire you   hurt or humiliation
                              ↓
                     They retaliate openly or
                     go underground
                              ↓
                     They take fewer initiatives
                                       or
                              ╱   ╲
              They become resigned   They leave

EFFECTS OF AGGRESSION ON ORGANIZATIONS

The organization as a whole is adversely affected by the previous consequences of aggression. When there are a number of people behaving
aggressively the effects are multiplied. In particular, the organization may lose
some talented and questioning people who, after a few early clashes, decide
they are not prepared to work in such an aggressive environment. The staff
who stay are likely to take fewer initiatives and risks, and to keep quiet about
their ideas or doubts.

A problem we have encountered in several organizations concerns one-way
aggressiveness from senior managers to junior managers. Here the dilemma is
for junior staff newly promoted to their first management job. They are
expected to continue being nonassertive (even deferential) to their aggressive
seniors, but also to become aggressive with their own staff. Unfortunately,
these junior managers find it difficult to suddenly swing to aggression because
all their working life they have behaved nonassertively.

An organization may also suffer when some of its managers behave
aggressively towards each other. This will result in more energy being put into
beating each other (often referred to as 'playing politics') and less into
cracking the problems they face. This may show itself in managers taking
decisions (such as extensive 'empire-building') that are in their own or their
department's interests but not in the interests of the organization.

Another problem occurs when large groups of people within organizations
behave aggressively towards each other. Perhaps the most publicized example
of this is trade unions and management, where the mutual aggression often
leads to polarization, which in turn leads to more aggression. Thus, not only
do more conflicts arise, but also these are often handled aggressively from
early on, because of the deeply entrenched positions taken up.

Such 'in-fighting' may leave less time for attending to customers' needs,
both immediate and longer-term. It is not uncommon for organizations to
find that, over time, their base in the market place becomes eroded.

12

So, there are many undesirable effects of aggression, not only for the people involved but also for the organization. Let us now look at what may be leading you or others to behave aggressively.

How you come to be aggressive

As we have already said, there are a number of short-term 'rewards' that, in spite of any longer-term undesirable effects, will reinforce your aggression. There may even be longer-term rewards for aggression, such as organizations either deliberately or unwittingly encouraging aggression by promoting managers who behave aggressively. This is likely to happen where aggressive managers move on after a couple of years before the longer-term effects of their aggression become apparent. In addition, there are reasons for aggression. We describe some of these in the following sections.

PERCEIVING SITUATIONS OR OTHER PEOPLE AS THREATENING

We said earlier that, if you feel threatened by a situation or by someone, then you may behave nonassertively. However, an alternative way to protect yourself in the face of threat is to 'hit out'; hence the saying 'attack is the best form of defence'.

The threat itself comes in several forms. It may be an *actual* attack from someone, for instance in a meeting a colleague saying: 'What on earth makes you think that'll work?—That's a crazy idea.' It may be a *perceived* attack. A good example of this is a person giving a presentation and being unsure of his material. He sees a 'genuine' question, to which he does not know the answer, as an attempt to show him up. He may well hit back with a sarcastic comment to hide his ignorance: 'If you'd been listening earlier, you wouldn't need to ask that.' The threat may come from an *anticipated* attack from someone. Let us suppose you have failed to meet a particular deadline. You expect to be taken to task by your manager in the review meeting next day. So you brace yourself for this and go into the meeting ready to go into the attack.

YOUR BELIEFS ABOUT AGGRESSION

If you believe that the only way to get results is to be aggressive, and you want to get results, then you will behave aggressively. Such a belief stems from seeing the world as a hostile place, in which the only way to survive is to 'get them before they get you'. We have come across a lot of managers who hold these beliefs as well as organizations that encourage managers in these beliefs.

It is a self-fulfilling prophecy that, if you behave aggressively towards staff and colleagues, then they are likely to behave aggressively in return. The spiral of aggression is set up, so that the world of work does indeed become a hostile place.

In addition, you may see nonassertion as the only alternative to aggression.

13

This leads you to make statements like 'Either you run your staff, or they run you.' You can see that you may survive in such a hostile environment by behaving nonassertively, but you reckon you will probably not progress. So you hold on to your aggressive behaviour. As we see it, the flaw in this thinking is that it denies or ignores the option of behaving assertively.

We do not deny that at times aggression can get results in the short run, but as we have seen, it usually has undesirable side effects associated with it. Our experience tells us that assertive behaviour can achieve equally good results in the short run without these undesirable side effects, and often better results in the long run.

EARLIER NONASSERTION

When you have been nonassertive about something for a period of time, frustration, hurt, or anger can build up within you until you are not prepared to stand it any longer. You express your anger or defiance aggressively, often blaming others for the results of your nonassertion: 'I'm sick and tired of your asking me to do the boring jobs.' Other people may be perplexed by the sudden outburst because they have not necessarily behaved any differently towards you. They are probably not aware that this was 'the last straw'.

Another common way in which nonassertion and aggression are linked is when you behave nonassertively towards people with greater authority, often stifling the frustration or anger you feel as a result. You may then express these feelings by behaving aggressively towards people over whom you have some authority. For instance, if you have taken on more work from your manager than your department can handle you may then behave aggressively to your subordinates when they complain of the impossible workload.

OVER-REACTING BECAUSE OF A PREVIOUS EXPERIENCE

Sometimes you respond to a present situation with emotions that are left over from a past incident. So, strong feelings of resentment towards a colleague resulting from an incident yesterday can lead you to make aggressive comments about him to another colleague today, e.g., 'Don't talk to me about Fred . . . .'

FAILING TO THINK RATIONALLY ABOUT YOURSELF

This can happen when you frequently compare yourself with others. Sometimes the comparisons you make will be exaggerated unfavourably against you and will lead you to feel jealousy or resentment against others. This will result in your behaving aggressively towards them, maybe making sarcastic remarks against a particularly competent member of staff. At other times the comparisons you make will be exaggerated in your favour and will lead you to boast to other people: 'I really took the whole show there.' You

14

might even criticize other people with negative comparison; for instance, 'How come you didn't get the same response I got from the customer?'

FAILING TO DEVELOP ASSERTIVE SKILLS

If the environment in which you work or have been brought up has encouraged you to use lots of aggressive behaviours, then these are the behaviours you become skilled at. (You may become expert at making people look small, or the master of the sarcastic aside.) You may develop, or may have lost through lack of practice, the skills to be successfully assertive.

So far in the chapter we have shown that both nonassertion and aggression have undesirable effects, mostly in the longer term. In spite of this, nonassertion and aggression will continue if reinforced by short-term effects. There are various ways to break the cycle, but probably the sensible starting point is to begin behaving more assertively (as outlined in Chapter 4, for instance), and so to experience pleasant effects of assertion. We examine these in the next section.

Why be more assertive?

The short answer to this is that we believe behaving more assertively will result in your being more effective in your job. This is because assertion tends to breed assertion, so people are more likely to keep working *with* you rather than *against* you. In turn, this makes it easier to get satisfactory outcomes to many of the situations you have to handle. Let us illustrate this by returning to the examples we have used at various stages in the chapter. Your boss has asked you to complete some additional work. You are the best person to do the work but you have no spare time. An assertive response would be: 'I appreciate that you would like this work completed by the end of the month. However, I don't see I can fit it in with our workload as it is at present.' As a result of this particular assertion we predict that the outcome of the situation will be that you agree to take on the boss's additional work and he agrees to make changes to the workload. Because you are the best person to do the work, we would regard this as a high-quality outcome.

In many other situations it will also be important to get outcomes that are of a high quality—solutions that are workable, procedures that can readily be implemented, agreements that are clearly understood. Below we list a number of situations from which you will probably want to get 'good' outcomes or results.

– Coping with an angry customer, without making promises you cannot keep
– Asking your manager for a regrading to reflect the extra responsibilities you have taken on
– Having to make important arrangements over the telephone with a colleague who goes on at great length and is difficult to pin down

- Conveying 'bad news' to senior management
- Saying 'No' to unreasonable requests from colleagues, staff, or senior managers
- Disagreeing with the views of others in a meeting, without causing resentment
- Carrying out an appraisal with a member of staff who believes he is ready for promotion when you do not think he is
- Chasing people up who have promised to do something for you as a favour and then have not done it
- Reaching agreement with a colleague who is behaving aggressively so that you feel you stood your ground without becoming aggressive in return

We believe that behaving assertively in these and other situations will help you achieve effective outcomes in these situations. These will contribute to your increasing your overall effectiveness. In addition, assertion has other benefits, some of which we explain in the following sections.

AN INCREASED CHANCE OF NEEDS BEING MET

If you are behaving more assertively, you are stating more clearly what your needs, wants, ideas, and opinions are. This by itself increases the chances that your needs will be met and your opinions taken into account.

At the same time, because assertion is about not ignoring or dismissing the needs and wants of others, you will encourage others to make their needs known. If there is no conflict between their needs and yours, then you have increased the chances that these too will be met. Where the needs that emerge are in conflict, then we believe assertive behaviour helps individuals to find solutions that are acceptable to both persons. More detail on this is given in Chapter 11.

GREATER CONFIDENCE IN YOURSELF

We do recognize, however, that in some instances your needs may not be fully met. Indeed, in some cases they may not be met at all. The important point here is that, even if this should happen, because you have made your needs or views known, you are more likely to feel 'OK' about yourself and the situation. Afterwards you will say to yourself such things as: 'I stood up to Helen, and said what I had to say in a reasonable manner.'

Feeling OK about a situation enables you to put it behind you as opposed to replaying it over and over in your mind ('I wish I'd spoken up. What I should have said was . . .'). This takes up valuable time and energy and leaves you with less confidence to face up to the next tricky situation.

Handling difficult situations to your satisfaction will lead you to say to yourself, 'I can get John to listen to my ideas' or 'I can talk to my staff about their performance when it is not up to par, without creating ill feeling between us.'

16

This will lead you to have a *healthy* regard for yourself, your skills and abilities. (This is not to be confused with boastfulness, e.g., 'I'm the best at . . .', which is aggression.) There is a snowball effect here in that behaving assertively leads to greater self-confidence, which in turn leads to more assertive behaviour.

GREATER CONFIDENCE IN OTHERS

Increased confidence about yourself helps you to recognize and accept the strengths of those who work with or for you, rather than being threatened by them. So you use the strength that a particular member of your staff has for giving presentations. At the same time you will be more open about their limitations. Thus, in delegating to them, for example, you would not do it in a reckless way, which ignores their lack of experience in this new area, but in a planned, realistic way that recognizes any limitation on their performance. Handling it in this way enables you to feel confident that the task will be carried out satisfactorily.

INCREASED RESPONSIBILITY FOR YOUR OWN BEHAVIOUR

Being more assertive involves you taking more responsibility for your own behaviour. This leads in turn to your being more in control of your behaviour. So you move away from blaming other people for your behaviour; you no longer say things like: 'I couldn't help myself. After he brought up the issue of overtime again, I just blew my top.'

Increasing your assertion leads you to recognize that you have more control over how you respond to such incidents than you previously thought. At the same time, you realize that if you 'cannot stop yourself' from responding with aggression in such situations, then you are handing control of your behaviour over to the other person. He begins to see that he only has to mention overtime to get you to 'blow your top'.

Initially you may doubt that you can learn to control your own behaviour. 'It's only natural to respond aggressively in such situations', you say. Our experience is that people can increase their control by the techniques described in this book.

TAKING MORE INITIATIVES

If you are to influence the environment in which you work, it is not enough just to react to situations as they occur. It is necessary and important to take initiatives to make or stop certain situations occurring. These intiatives may be small—for example, putting forward an idea in a meeting—or large—such as changing the flow of work through your department.

If you behave assertively you are more likely to take such initiatives, because you are not afraid of failure or of making a mistake. You do not want

17

to fail and will work hard to get it right. However, you recognize that from time to time an initiative will fail, but that you can acknowledge and cope with this failure. You do not let the risk of failure stop you taking the intiative as people behaving nonassertively do. Neither do you try and blame others or pretend that it was not a failure, as the aggressive person does.

A SAVING IN ENERGY

Because you are no longer preoccupied with not upsetting others (n.a.), and no longer so concerned about losing out (agg), you will be able to save yourself a lot of nervous energy. For instance, no longer will you be worrying about how to tell a member of staff that he has not got the promotion he was expecting, or planning how to get back at somebody who tried to show you up in a meeting yesterday.

You will also experience a reduction in stress and tension associated with getting results. For example, you will find taking decisions less stressful because you will be less concerned with what other people think and with the fear of making a mistake.

Using less energy in these negative ways leaves you more energy to use productively in other areas of your job.

Some concluding considerations

NO ONE IS LIKELY TO BEHAVE AGGRESSIVELY OR NONASSERTIVELY ALL THE TIME

Each person's behaviour at this moment is likely to be a mixture of the three options available. The size of the segments in the pie chart below will be different for different people. We may, however, be able to make certain generalizations. For example, in Figure 1.1 a pie chart representing managers'

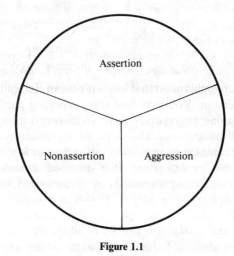

Figure 1.1

interactions with their senior managers will have a larger nonassertion segment than one representing their interactions with their staff. It follows that, strictly speaking, it is incorrect to talk of an aggressive or nonassertive person. We really prefer to say that he was behaving aggressively or nonassertively in that particular situation.

YOUR ASSERTION MAY BREAK DOWN IN DIFFICULT SITUATIONS

It is likely that for you and many people holding down a job in an organization the assertion segment of the pie chart in Figure 1.1 will certainly be substantial. You will be using assertive behaviours much of the time. It is during what you perceive to be difficult situations that the aggressive or nonassertive behaviours come to the fore. So being more assertive is about *spreading* your assertive behaviour into these difficult situations.

NONASSERTION AND AGGRESSION OFTEN COME FROM THE SAME SOURCE

Much evidence and our own experience suggests that both nonassertion and aggression spring from low-esteem. Your self-esteem is the evaluation that you make and hold about yourself. It is *your* judgement of *your* worth as a person. It is based upon the extent to which you believe yourself to be a competent, significant, likeable, and successful person.

If your self-esteem is low, then you will feel an uncomfortable degree of anxiety in certain situations. You will feel threatened by that situation and the people in it. When you feel threatened you either hit out (agg) or you 'turn into yourself' for protection (n.a.).

So the sequence is:

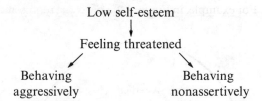

It is important to stress this point that low self-esteem can lead to aggression as well as to nonassertion. You may find this surprising particularly because many people behaving aggressively have an outward appearance of over-confidence and self-assuredness. This outward aggression is often a mask for the insecurity that comes from unhealthy self-regard or low esteem. You may have noticed how this mask can drop when someone stands up to this person. The aggression crumbles and is replaced by nonassertion, say in the form of excessive apologizing.

BEING ASSERTIVE IS DEALING WITH ISSUES WHEN THEY ARE SMALL

We believe that if you can deal with issues and problems when they are small, then you will have fewer of the 'big blow ups' that are so draining, and difficult to resolve. You will also be more successful in resolving these issues. Once problems have been around a while and grown in size and importance they are more difficult to resolve—not only because they are more complex, but also because the people involved have had more time to take up entrenched positions. So, for instance, dealing with a sarcastic comment as and when it is made may well save a more aggressive exchange later on.

In this chapter we have introduced the concepts of assertiveness. Many of the themes, like rights and negative feelings, will be developed in later chapters, as will practical applications of the concepts.

2. Recognizing assertive, nonassertive and aggressive behaviour

In the previous chapter we included definitions of ass, agg, and n.a. If you want to use more assertive behaviour (and at this point we will assume you do), then an essential step towards this is for you to be able to recognize when you and others are actually using ass, agg, or n.a. But the definitions we used were global statements about these three types of behaviour; they were only a start point in the process of recognizing the three types. So in this chapter we will make more specific distinctions between ass, agg, and n.a. For each of the three types we describe the *verbal* behaviour used and then give a recognition exercise for you to work through. Following this, we look at the *nonverbal* aspects of the three types.

Verbal aspects of behaviour

By this we mean *what* people say: the message they convey and the words they use. We are not here concerned with *how* people say it. So in the next three sections we describe the statements and questions people use for each of the three behaviour types and give examples of them.

VERBAL ASPECTS OF ASSERTION

Just to recap, assertive behaviour is standing up for your own rights, wants, needs, and beliefs without violating those of other people. So, people behaving assertively are likely to use the following:

– 'I' statements, like: 'I think. . .'; 'My idea is. . .'; 'I want. . .'; 'I'd like to. . .'; 'I prefer. . .'; 'I feel. . .'. These indicate that the person is speaking for himself rather than for some unidentified entity such as 'the department'. So: 'I'd like to change the procedure' rather than 'It would be a good idea to change the procedure'.
– Statements that are brief and to the point: 'I'd like to get started this week'. From this, it is clear what you want. By contrast, long rambling statements confuse the other person, leaving him unclear about what you want.
– Distinctions between fact and opinion: 'As I see it. . .'; 'My opinion is. . .'; 'My experience is different in that. . .'. This recognizes that things are not always 'black and white', 'good or bad', but that they can be different for different people. So: 'The system works well for me' rather than 'The system is good'.

- Explanations that can be distinguished from the rest of the speech: 'because next week there'll be lots of interruptions'. Reasons, causes, effects, etc., are 'labelled' with phrases like 'that was because. . .'; 'this will lead to. . .'; 'this is so that we can. . .'.
- Suggestions (for how the other person could proceed) that *do not* contain heavily weighted 'advice': 'How about tackling it this way. . .?'; 'Would it be practical to. . .'; 'Would you like to. . .'. These enable the other person to make up his own mind after evaluating the suggestions for himself.
- Constructive 'criticism', which states the facts of people's actions without attacking them as people: 'Colin, your reports have not been coming in on time.' There is no excessive blaming here or jumping to conclusions.
- Questions to find out the thoughts, opinions and wants of others: 'How does that fit in with your plans?'; 'What will this involve?' 'What are your thoughts on. . .'. More use is made of 'open-ended' questions (i.e., ones that require more than a yes/no answer) to get more information back. 'Leading' questions (that push the other person into making the 'approved' response) are avoided: 'You do delegate work, don't you?'
- Behaviours for getting round problems: 'Let's look for a way to overcome that', 'How can we get around that?' 'Shall we. . .?'

These words and phrases differ from ones that people use when they are being nonassertive or aggressive.

VERBAL ASPECTS OF NONASSERTION

As we have said, nonassertive behaviour is failing to stand up for your rights, needs, and wants, or doing so in ways that make it easy for other people to violate them. So, people behaving nonassertively are likely to use the following:

- Rambling statements—sometimes long and complex, sometimes tailing off at the end: 'I thought you might like to. . . er. . . well. . .'. These either take a circuitous route to mentioning the subject under discussion, or fail to mention it at all (perhaps in the hope that the other person will do so).
- Fill-in words and hesitant phrases: 'Uh'; '. . .you know what I mean'; 'well. . .like'; 'only'; 'just'; 'maybe'; 'er. . .erm'. These often show that the speaker is camouflaging the message or gathering courage to deliver it.
- Frequent justifications of themselves: 'I wouldn't normally mention this only. . .'; 'I was just going past your door so I thought I'd see whether. . .'. These justifications are often meant to weaken the impact of the speaker's behaviour and reduce the chances of other people perceiving it as 'bold'. They usually point to a confusion between assertiveness and aggressiveness.
- Profuse apologies, and statements 'seeking permission': 'I'm terribly sorry, I really didn't mean to. . .'; 'I'm very sorry to bother you'; 'I hope you don't mind but would it be all right if. . .'; 'Excuse me please, but can we. . .'. Many of these indicate confusion between politeness and nonassertion. It's polite

to apologize after spilling beer over someone's dress; it's n.a. to do so *profusely* like a 'whipped dog', or to apologize in advance for some anticipated 'misdemeanour'. People constantly 'seeking permission' have handed over control for themselves to others.

- Self-regulatory statements: 'I should'; 'I must'; 'I ought to get on with X'; 'I have to. . .'. These indicate that the person has handed over control to an outside force whom he feels duty bound to obey. The force may be parents, spouse, colleague, boss, department, etc.
- Few 'I' statements, and usually with qualifiers: 'It's only my opinion but. . .'; 'I think it will work, but I might be wrong'. These qualifiers down play the fact that the person is speaking for himself, and also make it less likely that others will challenge his view.
- Phrases that dismiss their own needs and wants: 'I could do with some extra time but it doesn't matter really'; '. . .but it's not important'; 'Yes, but don't worry, I'll manage'. These reduce the risk of an outright refusal which would be embarrassing or hurtful. They invite the other person to ignore the needs and wants.
- Phrases that put themselves down: 'I'm hopeless at this'; 'You know me, I seem to be useless at. . .'; 'I can't seem to. . .'. These often invite a denial and even a pat on the back from the other person. Sometimes the person using these phrases will wallow in self-despair instead of making changes that will overcome whatever deficiency exists.

People using the above statements would be raising issues and responding to other people, albeit tentatively or self-deprecatingly. In addition to this, people frequently behave nonassertively by saying *nothing*. They will fail to raise issues that concern them; they will keep quiet about their doubts and disagreements.

   The words and phrases used above contrast with ones that people use when they are being aggressive.

VERBAL ASPECTS OF AGGRESSION

Aggressive behaviour, as we have stated, is standing up for your own rights, needs, wants, and beliefs in ways that violate or ignore those of other people. So people behaving aggressively are likely to use the following:

- An excess of 'I' statements with heavy emphasis on the 'I' part: '*I* think it will work', '*My* view is that. . .' '*I'd* like. . .'. This emphasis infers that the speaker's view is more important, which deters other people from challenging it.
- Boastfulness: '*My* projects are *always* on time.' Here the negative comparison of other people is *implied*, at other times it is stated: '*I* never have any problems with this, not like *you*.'
- Opinions expressed as facts: 'That won't work'; 'Nobody wants to do that'; 'That procedure is useless'. These indicate that the person is speaking for

everyone, basing his judgement on his own experience and ignoring other people's experience.

- Threatening questions: 'Why on earth did you do *that*?'; 'Haven't you come up with a solution yet?' These unnerve the other person by 'putting him on the spot'. The questions turn an interaction into an inquisition.
- Requests in the form of instructions or even threats: 'You'd *better* do that'; 'I *want* that information *straightaway*'; 'That report *has* to be finished by tomorrow, or else'. A threat may be spoken or implied, but in any case the instructions alone mean that the person is trying to control the other person.
- Heavily weighted advice for how the other person could proceed: 'You should do it this way'; 'You must pull your socks up'; 'You ought'; 'You have to'. All these are quoting some hidden 'rule book' that controls the other person. They imply a moral judgement of 'bad', 'wrong', 'wicked' on whoever disobeys. Sometimes the advice is of the fatherly sort, with plenty of well-meant persuasion: 'If I were you. . .'; 'Why don't you. . .'. All of these suggestions, both fatherly and otherwise, reduce the chances of the other person evaluating the suggestions for himself and making up his own mind.
- Blame for past events, often with no constructive statements about change: 'It wouldn't have happened if you hadn't been so. . .'; 'You made a mess of that'; 'Well, I blame the youth/workers/management of today'; 'Your attitude is all wrong'. These generalized comments do not highlight specific cause and effects of behaviour. It is difficult for the other person to do anything about a general disorder like a 'mess' or an 'attitude'; and the excessive blaming makes it unlikely that he would want to anyway.
- Assumptions about people and events: 'I don't suppose you've done X'; 'Presumably you won't want much time for this'; 'Production missed the deadlines, as usual'. These assumptions stem from notions of 'I know you better than you do' or 'These people are always the same'.
- Sarcasm and similar statements: 'You must be joking'; 'That's only *your* opinion'; 'That's rubbish'. These put the other person down by dismissing his opinions, suggestions or needs.

In the last three sections we have described the verbal aspects of ass, n.a., and agg. You have probably been saying various things to yourself like: 'Hm, that sounds like me' or 'My boss/colleague says things like that'. This is fine from our point of view, because it means you are probably keen to go on now and spot examples of ass, n.a., and agg behaviours as they actually occur. But before doing this, if you want to make sure you can distinguish the three types of behaviour, on paper at least, then work through the recognition exercise, Table 2.2. As a 'memory jogger' for doing this, the chart in Table 2.1 restates the verbal content of the three types of behaviour in a convenient form. At the end it gives an example of the same issue being raised in the three different ways: ass, n.a., and agg.

24

Table 2.1. Summary of verbal aspects of behaviour

	Nonassertive	Assertive	Aggressive
Verbal content	– Long, rambling statements – Fill-in words: 'maybe' – Frequent justifications – Apologies and 'permission seekers' – 'I should', 'I ought' – Few 'I' statements (often qualified) – Phrases that dismiss own needs: 'not important really' – Self put-downs 'I'm hopeless'	– Statements that are brief, clear and to the point – 'I' statements: 'I'd like' – Distinctions between fact and opinion – Suggestions not weighted with 'advice' – No 'shoulds' nor 'oughts' – Constructive 'criticism' without blame or assumptions – Questions to find out the thoughts, opinions, wants of others – Ways for getting round problems	– Excess of 'I' statements – Boastfulness: '*My*' – Opinions expressed as facts – Threatening questions – Requests as instructions or threats – Heavily weighted advice in the form of 'should' and 'ought' – Blame put on others – Assumptions – Sarcasm and other put-downs

Background to example

A colleague rings up when you are working on a report that you particularly want to finish. He says he wants to talk about next week's safety meeting. You prefer to discuss the matter later in the day.

	Nonassertive	Assertive	Aggressive
Your response	'Oh, I hope you don't mind but I'm a bit busy at the moment. Would it be all right if I rang you back later this afternoon?'	'Fine. I'm happy to talk about the safety meeting, but right now I'd like to finish this report. How about my ringing you back later this afternoon?'	'You can't expect me to think about a safety meeting. I'm in the middle of a report. You'll have to ring me back later.'

Recognition exercise: assertive, nonassertive and aggressive behaviours

The exercise in Table 2.2 contains 20 examples, each with a description of a situation followed by a response. You are asked to state whether each response is assertive (ass) nonassertive (n.a.), or aggressive (agg).

There is space for you to write your answer in the *right*-hand column. The correct answer for each response is given in the *left*-hand column, on the *line below*. This enables you to check your own answer before moving on to the next example. This way you reduce the risk of making the same mistake more than once throughout the exercise. It is usually best to reveal only one example at a time, covering up the answer until you are ready to check it.

If you don't see why a response has been answered the way it has, please note this and check it out with the explanations we give at the end of the exercise (Table 2.3) or look back through the chapter at the detailed descriptions and examples.

Table 2.2. Recognition exercise

Answer	Situation	Response	Your answer
	1. The date is being set for the next meeting of the committee of which you are a member. You are keen to attend but the proposed date accepted by everyone else, means you cannot attend. When the chairman says 'Is that OK for everyone, then?' You say:	'Well, all right, as it seems to be convenient to everyone else.'	
n.a.	2. A colleague asks you for a lift home. It's inconvenient to you, as you are late already and the drive will take you out of your way. You say:	'I'm about 20 minutes late so I won't be able to take you home. If it helps I can drop you off at the nearest bus stop.'	
ass	3. You're having trouble getting started on a report. You can't see a logical starting point. You say to a colleague:	'I'm pretty useless at writing reports. I can't really see how to even start it. I must be getting old!'	
n.a.	4. Your boss asks what went wrong when you were installing a new machine for a customer. You say:	'You wasted a lot of my time! You never even *told* me he didn't have the area ready.'	
agg	5. A subordinate interrupts you when you are making an important call to a supplier. You say:	'I'd like to finish this phone call, then I'll be happy to answer your question.'	
ass	6. Your secretary is arranging your diary for the day. She		

26

Table 2.2 (*continued*)

Answer	Situation	Response	Your answer
	6. (*continued*) asks you 'What time will you be back in the office?' You say:	'When you see me walk in.'	
agg	7. A colleague hears you dealing with an awkward customer. Afterwards he praises the way you handled it. You say:	'Well, I only really came in at the end.'	
n.a.	8. You sat in on a presentation given by one of your staff. You felt it was highly successful. You say:	'I think that was a really good presentation. I particularly liked the way you made the material interesting.'	
ass	9. One of your staff is going to visit a client who is well known as a 'slippery character'. You know your subordinate is hesitant in his dealings with people. You say to him:	'You've *got* to stand up to him, Pete. Tell him what's acceptable to us. You *mustn't* let him get away with airy-fairy nonsense, like *last* time.'	
agg	10. A colleague has just produced a good work plan for his department. You'd like his help with one for your department. You say:	'That work plan, you produced is a good approach. Will you be able to spend half an hour working on one with me for my department?'	
ass	11. A member of staff tells you she is wanting to take responsibility for some of the enquiries. You say:	'What on earth for? You know jolly well you're struggling to keep up with the filing—without doing extra work.'	
agg	12. A salesman has been pushing hard for you to buy a piece of equipment. You are not too sure; besides, you had thought of looking at several makes before deciding. You say:	'Well, I suppose it's more or less what I'm looking for. I was going to look at other makes, but perhaps this will be OK.'	

Table 2.2 (*continued*)

Answer	Situation	Response	Your answer
n.a.	13. A colleague in another department has volunteered your services without consulting you to help a junior manager draw up his financial return! You say:	'What a nerve! Why didn't you ask me first? There's no way I can help out. I'm up to my eyes as it is. He'll have to work it out for himself like the rest.'	
agg	14. Your boss wants Pete, your subordinate, to carry out a survey for her over the next two weeks. You really prefer Steve, another subordinate, to do the survey. You say:	'Well, I don't know. Pete has just started a job for the Packer firm, but perhaps he could be taken off that. Steve won't be so good at the Packer job but I suppose I could always help him out.'	
n.a.	15. A colleague agreed to come to a special meeting and then failed to turn up. You ring him and say:	'Dave, I understood you were coming to the meeting. I would have liked you to be there. What happened?'	
ass	16. One of your staff (you don't know which one) forgot to list details of a customer's receipt. You are aware of this and say to your staff:	'One of you forgot to note the details of Williams's receipt. I don't care who it is, I want it put right, straight away.'	
agg	17. Your boss has sent a memo saying that no more business visits must be made without his prior agreement. You are unhappy with this and you say to him:	'Colin, I'm not happy with the new arrangement. The way I see it, it takes away my professional judgement. I'd like to discuss this with you.'	
ass	18. A subordinate has asked for time off to visit a sick relative at a time when the department is working frantically to finish the monthly returns. You say:	'I hope you won't think I'm being mean, but Mr Cross will not like you to take time off tomorrow. I'm very sorry.'	

Table 2.2 (*continued*)

Answer	Situation	Response	Your answer
n.a.	19. Your boss asks you to attend a meeting. The last time you went it wasn't relevant to your department so you don't want to go. You say:	'I'm really busy this week with schedules, I don't think I'll have time to go.'	
n.a.	20. You're about to do some copying when a fellow employee who often asks you to do her copyings says: 'Can you just run off 30 of these for me?' You say:	'I'm usually happy to help you out, but I don't want to spend time on extra copying this morning.'	
ass			

If, with some of the examples in Table 2.2, you are wondering why we gave the answers we did, the comments in Table 2.3 (page 30) will explain our thinking.

If you have worked through the examples in Table 2.2, or as a result of your experiences to date, you might be saying 'But isn't it *how* you say things that determines whether they come across as assertive, nonassertive or aggressive?' The answer is both Yes and No.

Let us deal with the 'No' first of all. Supposing (as in example 3 in the table) you say things like: 'I'm pretty useless at writing reports'; then we see this as putting yourself down. It may be true, for instance, that when writing reports your language is not fluent, your arguments disorganized, but this does not necessarily add up to your being 'useless'. This would be understating your abilities—in our terms, behaving n.a. Alternatively (as in example 11), you might say to a subordinate something along the lines of: 'What on earth for? You know jolly well. . .'. Then we regard this as dismissing the other person, denying her right to have wants and views that are different from your own—in other words, behaving agg. With these examples, we convey a message that would be more or less unchanged no matter *how* we say them. It is the words themselves that make these and many other examples into n.a. or agg.

But 'Yes' sometimes it *does* depend on *how* we say things as to whether they are ass, agg, or n.a. Try saying the following statement (example 5) to yourself

29

Table 2.3. Comments on answers in recognition exercise

Ex. no.	Ans.	Comment
3	n.a.	Putting yourself down—helplessness
4	agg	Blaming, jumping to conclusions (the boss may not have had the information)
6	agg	Sarcastic; ignores her need to know; you may not have the answer, but this doesn't make the question invalid
7	n.a.	Selling yourself short (also, incidentally, has the effect of devaluing the person's praise)
9	agg	Giving heavily weighted advice
10	ass	Straight acknowledgement of the colleague's work. Not pleading or putting yourself down; nor instructing him to give time to you
11	agg	Dismissing subordinate's wants, questioning her judgement
16	agg	'Straightaway' has an implied threat of 'or else'
18	n.a.	Not taking any responsibility for the decision; apologizing
19	n.a.	Not 'coming clean'; giving excuse rather than real reason

several times, each time putting the emphasis on different words or pausing from time to time. For instance,

1. '*I'd* like to finish this *phone* call; *then* I'll be happy to answer your *question*.'
2. '*I'd like* to finish this *phone call*; then I'll be *happy* to answer your *question*.'
3. 'I'd. . . like to. . . finish this. . . phone call, then I'll. . . be happy to. . . answer your. . . question.'

Recognizing the limitations of written words, we have tried to portray no. 1 as agg, no. 2 as ass, and no. 3 as n.a. Whether you picked up these intended distinctions or not, you probably noticed considerable differences in the message that came across as you said the same statement to yourself in several ways. These different messages were conveyed not as a result of the words themselves (these were unchanged), but as a result of the differences in *how* you *said* the words—the emphasis, the tone of voice, the hesitancies. These are examples of what we will call *nonverbal* behaviour. 'Ah,' you may be saying, 'I've seen television programmes about head-scratching, ear-pulling and the like, but what does it all mean? Is there some deep significance in every twitch and gesture?' There may well be, but many of them will not be relevant to us here. We are concerned only with those nonverbal behaviours that go to make up ass, n.a., and agg behaviour and particularly the ones that enable us to increase our assertiveness. Let us look at these in more detail.

Nonverbal aspects of ass, agg and n.a.

By this we mean all the observable aspects of behaviour that accompany speech, apart from the words themselves. We include both audible and visible aspects, and the ones we have found to be important are the following:

Voice	The tone: sarcastic or sincere; warm or cold; rich and expressive or dull and flat
	The volume: shouting; barely audible; or medium volume
Speech	Slow, hesitant, fast, jerky, abrupt, or steady even pace
Facial expression	Brow: wrinkled or smooth
	Eyebrows: raised, lowered, or level
	Jaw: set firm or relaxed
Eye contact	Whether the speaker looks at other people or the surroundings and for how long
Body movement	Movement with individual parts of the body, e.g., head, hands
	Movement and position of the whole body

WHY NONVERBAL BEHAVIOURS ARE IMPORTANT TO ASSERTIVENESS

We have already mentioned that some statements can be said in different ways and that it is the nonverbal behaviours (tone of voice, emphasis, etc.) that determine whether these statements come across as ass, agg, or n.a. But more important than this, for people who want to increase their assertiveness, is the notion that *nonverbal behaviours can undermine potentially assertive words*. Let us illustrate what we mean by this.

Suppose a colleague says the following potentially assertive statement to you: 'I'd like to hear your thoughts on X.' He then looks at you with an open expression on his face, relaxed, and waiting for you to talk. You would be clear from all this that he wanted to listen carefully to your ideas. But suppose that, after making the statement, he folded his arms tightly across his chest, turned his body slightly away from you, stared at you with his chin thrust out and with his jaw tightly set. Would you still be certain that he was going to listen to you without pre-judging your ideas? Probably not.

So nonverbal behaviour can detract from and even override the verbal behaviour. If you want to behave assertively, you need to get the nonverbal aspects *in line* with the verbal aspects. If they are in line they give emphasis to your verbal assertions and increase the likelihood that your behaviour will come across to others as assertive.

We describe the nonverbal aspects associated with ass, agg, and n.a. in Table 2.4 and in the sections that follow. However, if you are not sure how aware you are of nonverbal behaviour generally, it is a good idea to look out for the ones we have described so far before going into further detail. The next time you are in a pub or at work try observing a couple of people holding a conversation you are not involved in. Or when you find yourself stuck with a boring television programme take your own natural break and notice the nonverbal behaviours of the participants (particularly fascinating if you turn the sound down).

A word of caution

A single example say of 'finger pointing' does not necessarily add up to aggressive behaviour. In order to decide whether a behaviour is ass, agg, or n.a. we might need to look at the other nonverbal behaviours being used. The examples in Table 2.4 are meant only as guidelines; many of them may well not be a part of your nonverbal 'repertoire', or you may have ones that are different from these. What is important is that you select the nonverbal behaviours that you believe are most preventing you from increasing your assertiveness and work at bringing these into your conscious control. In our experience no one has ever increased her assertiveness by globally bringing her nonverbal behaviours into line. But people have, for instance, improved their fluency by practising speaking slowly yet firmly, emphasizing key words.

Table 2.4. Nonverbal aspects of n.a., ass and agg

	Nonassertive	Assertive	Aggressive
Voice	– Sometimes wobbly – Tone may be singsong or whining – Over-soft or over-warm – Often dull and in monotone – Quiet, often drops away at end	– Steady and firm – Tone is middle range, rich and warm – Sincere and clear – Not over-loud or quiet	– Very firm – Tone is sarcastic, sometimes cold – Hard and sharp – Strident, often shouting, rises at end
Speech pattern	– Hesitant and filled with pauses – Sometimes jerks from fast to slow – Frequent throat-clearing	– Fluent, few awkward hesitances – Emphasizes key words – Steady, even pace	– Fluent, few awkward hesitances – Often abrupt, clipped – Emphasizes blaming words – Often fast

Table 2.4 (*continued*)

	Nonassertive	Assertive	Aggressive
Facial expression	– 'Ghost' smiles when expressing anger, or being criticized – Eyebrows raised in anticipation (e.g., of rebuke) – Quick-changing features	– Smiles when pleased – Frowns when angry – Otherwise 'open' – Features steady, not wobbling – Jaw relaxed but not 'loose'	– Smile may become 'wry' – Scowls when angry – Eyebrows raised in amazement/ disbelief – Jaw set firm – Chin thrust forward
Eye Contact	– Evasive – Looking down	– Firm but not a 'stare-down'	– Tries to stare down and dominate
Body movements	– Hand-wringing – Hunching shoulders – Stepping back – Covering mouth with hand – Nervous movements which detract (shrugs and shuffles) – Arms crossed for protection	– Open hand movements (inviting to speak) – 'Measured pace' hand movements – Sits upright or relaxed (not slouching or cowering) – Stands with head held up	– Finger pointing – Fist thumping – Sits upright or leans forward – Stands upright head 'in air' – Strides around (impatiently) – Arms crossed (unapproachable)

ADDITIONAL NOTES

You may already have a sufficient picture of the different nonverbal behaviours, in which case we suggest you skip the following comments.

Speech pattern
'Emphasizes key words' (ass) means speaking certain words slowly, firmly and expressively, but not thumping them hard. The sorts of words to emphasize would mostly be nouns and verbs that we want people to visualize or remember; e.g., 'I *think* the programme meets our *needs* but I'd *like* to take *two days* to study it in *detail*.'

Facial expression

'Ghost' smiles (n.a.) are the smiles that fleet across a person's face when they are under attack, or when they are criticizing the other person.

A 'wry' smile (agg) is the sort that accompanies sarcasm, when the mouth turns up at the corners.

'Quick changing features' (n.a.) are where the face changes quickly from smiling to frowning to jaw dropping loose within the same sentence. It gives the impression that the person has no control over the facial expression.

Eye contact

This is one of the ways you regulate conversation. Have you noticed on the telephone how difficult it is to know whether the other person has finished speaking? You both need eye contact to tell each other when to come in, what each other's reactions are, what has been understood. You also need to look away from time to time, to collect your thoughts or to visualize things.

Body movements

In a sense, these are the way the body summarizes its behaviour. So with n.a. there is a curling up in *protection from* the 'world'; with ass there is a *standing up to face* the 'world'; and with agg there is a leaning forward in a point of *attack against* the world.

Summary

In this chapter we have said:
- Certain words and phrases are likely to be seen as assertive, nonassertive, or aggressive.
- Certain nonverbal behaviours are associated with assertion, nonassertion, and aggression.
- Nonverbal behaviours need to be in line with verbal behaviours in order to give emphasis to the verbal assertiveness.
- Increased assertiveness comes about by concentrating on one specific aspect of verbal or nonverbal behaviour at a time.

3. Rights!

You may well be familiar with the word 'rights', for instance in the context of company appraisals, where individuals often have the 'right' to appeal against a particular performance rating. Rights also occur in industrial relations, with management claiming the 'right' to manage and trade unions claiming the 'right' to be consulted. You may feel uneasy with the word 'rights' because it is often associated, especially in the latter context, with confrontation and aggression. But this need not be so. The problem lies not with the *concept* of rights as such, so much as with the *way people stand up* for their rights. Indeed, the dictionary definition, and the one we use, defines a right as simply 'something to which you are entitled'. Rights are a central issue to assertiveness. This is because our definition of assertiveness talks of standing up for your rights, wants, needs, and feelings without denying the rights, wants, needs, and feelings of others.

So the aim of this chapter is to enable you to be clear about the rights involved in any situation you may encounter. We look at why rights are important to assertiveness, some examples of general rights and where they come from, followed by specific rights and responsibilities within a job.

Why rights are important to assertiveness

Rights are important because they are one of the bases for deciding whether *other people* are behaving aggressively, nonassertively or assertively towards you. Quite simply, if you do not know what your rights are then you will find it difficult to judge whether other people are violating those rights. Let us suppose your manager comes to you insisting that you forgo one of your four holiday weeks. Now, it so happens that you know you have the right to four holiday weeks, so you can judge that your manager, by being insistent, is violating your rights—he is behaving aggressively. When you are able to make this sort of judgement, you can go on and decide whether and how to stand up for your rights.

A second reason why rights are important is that *not* being clear on them makes it more difficult for *you* to behave assertively. Have you ever found yourself
– Hesitating about raising an issue?
– Having decided to raise an issue but being unsure about 'how far to push' it?
– Being unsure of your ground but blustering your way through nonetheless?
One manager told us of the time he returned a new but faulty tyre to the garage supplying it. The supplier said that if he wanted a replacement tyre free of charge he would have to wait for one from the manufacturers. Alternatively,

they could fit one but would have to charge for the tyre. At this point the manager was unsure where he stood, so he reluctantly agreed to have a tyre from the manufacturer, which meant waiting at least a week. What happened here was that the manager was not clear whether he had the right to a free replacement tyre from the supplier or only from the manufacturer. Because of this he ended up dropping the issue (with some feelings of regret), and behaving nonassertively. So being clear on your rights and the rights of other people in any situation enables you to decide: whether other people are violating your rights, whether you are violating their rights, whether to raise a particular issue and how far to go.

At this point you may well be saying 'Fine, but what are my rights in any situation?' Many of the answers we would give to this will in turn lead you to ask a further question: 'But who says so?' So in the next section we propose to deal with the 'who says so' question, saying something of where 'general' rights come from. Then in the following two sections we consider what your 'general' and 'job' rights might be.

Where do 'general' rights come from?

By 'general' rights we mean rights that affect your dealings with work colleagues, family, friends, neighbours, and shopkeepers. We find it useful to think in terms of three major sources of general rights:

1. The rights enshrined in the laws of the land
2. The rights you come to accept as a result of your experiences
3. The rights you have in the area of assertiveness

RIGHTS CONFERRED BY THE LAW OF THE LAND
In the tyre example in the previous section the supplier was behaving aggressively (however unwittingly) because he was violating the right of the customer, as set out in English law covering the sale of goods. In this case, the manager had the right to have the faulty tyre replaced free of charge by the supplier. In a country where the laws are different the manager might not have had this right. Most laws are designed to maintain or establish a balance in people's dealings with each other, e.g., race relations, sex discrimination, etc. Many laws come about as a result of groups of people *believing* that they have certain rights which are being ignored. These rights then become enshrined in the law. Let us now look at the second type of 'general' rights.

RIGHTS YOU HAVE COME TO ACCEPT AS A RESULT OF YOUR EXPERIENCES
These form a part of what we will call your *belief system*, which consists of all the things you *believe* in and hold to be of *value*. It will include your religious and political beliefs as well as your beliefs, for instance, about the human race,

how other people should be treated, about the most effective way to manage, about yourself. Others cannot know what is in your belief system (unless you tell them); all they can do is deduce some of its contents from the opinions and ideas you put forward and the behaviours you use. For instance, if you consult staff about decisions that affect them, then people might deduce from this you hold a belief that consulting staff is important.

Your belief system has been built up over the years and its contents affected by the experiences you have had, and the way you have interpreted those experiences. Suppose that in the past you have put forward ideas and other people have reacted adversely to these ideas, saying things like: 'whatever for?'; 'that won't work'; 'what nonsense'. Your *interpretation* of these experiences may well lead you to *believe* that your ideas are not as good as other people's. In turn, this belief will affect the *rights* you give yourself. So you may not give yourself the right to put forward your ideas and have them considered. This will lead you to hold back on your suggestions or to let them pass if they are ignored.

On the other hand, if in the past other people have reacted to your ideas with phrases like: 'Great idea', 'Why didn't I think of that?' etc., then you might well come to believe that your ideas are always better than other people's. In so doing you may start to deny other people the right to put forward their ideas. You will give yourself the right not only to put your ideas forward but also to push them very hard, even in the face of disagreements from others.

So as you can see, a pattern is emerging along the lines of Figure 3.1.

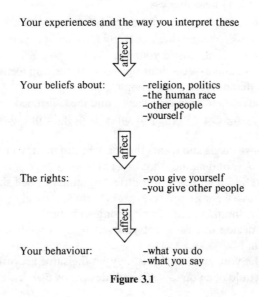

Figure 3.1

RIGHTS YOU HAVE WITHIN THE AREA OF ASSERTIVENESS

These derive from various humanistic beliefs such as 'all people are equal'; 'all people are entitled to freedom'. They are similar to the statements underpinning the constitutions of many countries and the Universal Declaration of Human Rights.

'All people are equal'

This is not to say that all people are the *same*, but rather that, regardless of race, colour, creed, background, or behaviour, all people are of equal *value* as human beings. Thus your colleague may put forward *different ideas* from yours (some might say 'better ideas'): this does not mean that he is a *better person* than you, or a more valuable person; it merely means that he is different.

'All people are entitled to freedom'

This is to say, all people are free to do and be what they like provided they do not affect others, taking away their freedom of choice. So, for instance, you are free to listen to your transistor on the beach provided you do not inflict that choice on others who prefer not to listen.

As with any belief system, an assertive belief system affects the rights you give yourself and others, which in turn affects your behaviour.

So having considered three major sources of rights, we will now look at what general rights you might have within the framework of assertiveness.

Your general rights in assertiveness

The following list contains some of the general rights that are available to you under 'assertiveness'. We see them as being important if you want to behave assertively in many situations in your life.

– The right to have and express your opinions, views, and ideas which may or may not be different from other people's
– The right to have these opinions, views, and ideas listened to and respected (not necessarily agreed with or put on a 'pedestal', but accepted as being valid for you)
– The right to have needs and wants that may be different from other people's
– The right to *ask* (not demand) that others respond to your needs and wants
– The right to refuse a request without feeling guilty or selfish
– The right to have feelings and to express them assertively if you so choose
– The right to be 'human', e.g., to be wrong sometimes
– The right to decide not to assert yourself (e.g., to choose not to raise a particular issue)
– The right to be your own self: this may be the same as, or different from, what others would like you to be (it includes choosing friends, interests etc.)

– The right to have others respect your rights

Underlying all this is *the right to be assertive*.

OVERLAP OF RIGHTS

There is likely to be some overlap in the rights we have outlined above, and those tumbling out from your own belief system. Where this is so they increase the chances that you will behave assertively in situations where these rights are involved.

DIFFERENCES IN RIGHTS

There may well be some rights in our list that you do not at present have in yours. This may be because some of the beliefs you hold are in conflict with the beliefs underpinning assertiveness. For instance, if you believe that your role in life is to serve others then you may not find it easy to accept, say, the right to refuse a request without feeling guilty or selfish.

There may also be some rights in your list that do not occur in ours. You may need to check back to your belief system to check these out. For example, if you believe that people (especially ones who disagree with you) are stupid, then you will probably give yourself the right to dictate to them. If you believe that people who put you down are bad or wicked, then you will give yourself the right to 'punish' them, or to 'get your own back'.

An assertive belief system, as we see it, does not include the right to violate other people's rights, even when they have violated your rights. But it does include the right to stand up for your own rights when these are being violated by other people, and to do so assertively.

ACCEPTANCE OF RIGHTS

Now, it is one thing to *understand* the above rights and even to *agree* that they probably are your rights. But this does not necessarily mean that you will *act* upon those rights. You can agree you have the right to ask for a reduced price on the carpet you are purchasing, but this does not mean you will actually do it, or do it assertively. In order for you to *act* upon your rights you need to really *accept* them.

You can test whether you really accept a particular right by asking yourself:
– Do I drop my assertiveness at any early sign of resistance?'
– 'After an assertion do I feel guilt or regret, or am I wondering if I did the right thing?'
– 'How often do I have to keep reminding myself I have this right?'
– 'Do I have to steel myself to exercise this right?'
You may find it useful at this point to go back through the list of general rights and identify which of these rights, if any, you have difficulty in accepting. Remember, accepting means being willing to stand up for them in the face of

resistance from others. For those you have difficulty in accepting, ask yourself:
– Why might this be so (e.g., is it in conflict with one of your beliefs—what experiences, and with whom, have resulted in this reluctance to accept)?
– What are the effects on your work, your social life, and your relations with others if you do not accept this right?
Answering these questions may in itself move you some way towards accepting the right in question. For any that are still in doubt you need to say things to yourself like: 'I *do* have the right to . . .' or 'I *do* give myself the right to . . .'

Job rights

We have identified some of the general rights that people can accept in their dealings with others; this section now deals with rights as they apply to a specific area—your job. Job rights may vary according to the job you do and will come from several sources:

1. The rights enshrined in the law of the land
2. The rights formally acknowledged in the policies of an organization
3. The rights between you and the people you work with

THE RIGHTS ENSHRINED IN THE LAW OF THE LAND
These have grown significantly in the last 20 years, so you now have the right to a contract of employment, to redundancy payment, to have safe working conditions, and so on. At any one time you may not be clear about the details of these rights. What you are aware of is that you do have rights in these areas, so if you suspect they are being infringed then you find out the detail prior to taking a stand.

THE RIGHTS ACKNOWLEDGED IN THE POLICIES OF AN ORGANIZATION
Some companies do more than meet the minimum legal requirements in aspects such as redundancy or holidays; their policies give employees additional rights. As well as this, some organizations develop policies not covered by government legislation, for example:
– The right to an appraisal of job performance at least once a year
– The right to a certain amount of time off in lieu
– The right to study for certain recognized qualifications in company time without loss of pay
Again, you may not be clear on the detail of these rights but you know where you can get such detail.

THE RIGHTS BETWEEN YOU AND THE PEOPLE YOU WORK WITH
For our purposes, these constitute the most important category of rights

40

within your job. We say this because they are the ones that influence your behaviour in most of the day-to-day situations you encounter. Some of these rights may be clearly understood, agreed, and accepted between you and the people you work with and for. This would be true, for instance, of rights stemming from your job description, where you might have the right, say, to make expenditures up to a certain amount. Other rights may not be clear to you or agreed between you and other people. Until they are agreed, it would be unwise to consider them as 'rights'. The list below includes the more common rights that many people believe they may have in their jobs:

– The right to be clear on what is expected of me
– The right to know how my manager sees my performance
– The right to get on with my job in my own way once objectives and constraints have been agreed
– The right to make mistakes from time to time
– The right to have a say/veto in selecting the people who work for me
– The right to expect work of a certain standard from my staff
– The right to criticize the performance of a member of staff when it falls below the required standard
– The right to be consulted about decisions that affect me
– The right to take decisions about matters that affect my department or area of work
– The right to refuse unreasonable requests (but see the comment on job descriptions below)

There may be some conflict between the above job rights and the ones you have that derive from your company's policies, your contract of employment, and your job description. Where this is so, the latter three sorts of rights take priority over the ones we have listed. This is because (presumably) you agreed to them when you took on your job.

Lack of clarity on rights

We may have given the impression that the rights between you and the people you work with are clearly identified and agreed. This is not always the case. Let us give an example of this and show what happened as a result.

Eric, the department manager, informed Geoff, one of his staff, that he had decided to make changes to the future workload. This was the first Geoff had heard of it, and he was annoyed that, once again, Eric had not consulted him before making the changes.

GEOFF: 'I'm pretty unhappy about that. It will involve me in doing more analysis work and that will clash with the other projects I'm doing.'
ERIC: 'Well that may be, but the work is changing and we've got to respond to it.'
GEOFF: 'What about getting Bob to do some of the analysis work?'
ERIC: 'He'll be up to his eyes in it, so he won't be able to help out.'

41

Geoff left the issue at this point although he felt dissatisfied with the outcome. Afterwards he realized that he was not annoyed about the changes as such, but at not being consulted about them. He had not said to Eric something along the lines of 'I'd like to be consulted on this in advance because changes in workload mean that I end up having to do a lot of reshuffling.' This would have been a statement in support of what he saw as his right to be consulted, which was really the underlying issue. But, as so often happens, the discussion dealt only with the more surface problem (in this case, the desirability of the changes in workload). Because the underlying issue, of whether Geoff has the right to be consulted before changes are made to his workload, has not been resolved, the problem is likely to re-occur.

So, lack of clarity about rights can affect your behaviour in a situation, the outcome of the situation, as well as your feelings about the outcome. In any situation where your rights are unclear, there are a number of steps you can take to clarify these.

Before a situation that you are about to face, ask yourself:
– 'What are my rights?'
– 'What are the other person's rights?'
– 'Does he accept my rights?'
– 'Do I accept his rights?'

During a situation in which you believe the other person has infringed your rights, but where these may not be clearly agreed between you,
– Step back from the detail of the situation.
– State what you see as your right (maybe not using the word 'right' but a phrase such as 'I'd like to be consulted on this in advance').
– Check that the other person agrees to this right.

So far, we have looked at what might be *your* general and job rights, but you might be feeling that rights could easily become a bit one-way. When this happens it contributes to the confusion in some people's minds between assertion and aggression. Thus we now want to consider the other side of the rights issue: responsibilities.

Rights and responsibilities

If you want to be seen as assertive rather than aggressive in standing up for your rights it is crucial to accept the *responsibilities* that go with rights. Table 3.1 gives some suggestions for responsibilities that accompany some of the job rights we mentioned earlier. If you fail to accept these responsibilities it makes it more difficult for other people to accept that you have the rights in the first place.

OVERRIDING RESPONSIBILITIES
– If you want to stand up for your rights *assertively*, then you have the

Table 3.1. Rights and responsibilities

Rights	Responsibilities
– To be allowed to get on with your job in your own way once objectives and constraints have been clarified	– To abide by these constraints – To use your time productively in working towards these objectives
– To have a say in selecting the people who are to work for you	– Not to abuse this right for personal ends (e.g., vetoing a person whom you see as a threat to you in your job)
– To make a mistake from time to time	– To acknowledge a mistake rather than blaming others – To put it right – To learn from it, i.e., not repeat it
– To expect work of a certain standard from the people working for you	– To let people know what the standards are
– To criticize the performance of your staff when it falls below this standard	– To do it assertively – To recognize there may be legitimate reasons for this

responsibility to be selective about the rights you do decide to stand up for. Sticking rigidly to what you believe your rights to be, or taking a stand every time your rights have been infringed however slightly, may all be counter-productive.

– You have the responsibility to accept and respect the rights of others. It would be easy to become so concerned about your own rights that you lose sight of other people's. We look at this in more detail in the following section.

Other people's rights

The emphasis so far in this chapter has been upon your accepting your own rights. This is important if you are to behave assertively rather than nonassertively. On the other hand, if you are to behave assertively and not aggressively, it is crucial to recognize and accept the rights of others. So for the *general* rights mentioned earlier, if you accept them for yourself, do you also accept that other people have them? We are using the word 'accept' as before, in that it is not just an intellectual acknowledgement but a commitment that influences your behaviour. Do you accept that *all* other people or only *some* other people have them? If only some, who are the some and why are you denying these rights to others?

With job rights, there may be differences between yours and the people working for you. However, if you have given them the same general rights as yourself, and as you are working for the same organization, then it is likely you will hold a lot of job rights in common. For example, if you give yourself

43

the right to make a mistake from time to time, can you deny this right to people working for you? Accepting that they do have this right, and replaying it over in your mind when people make an error, will help you to raise the issue assertively with them, rather than aggressively.

Accepting and respecting the rights of others in this way is a major responsibility that anyone has who wants to behave assertively. Accepting this responsibility not only encourages others to respect your rights, but also helps to ensure that your assertion is really assertion and not aggression masquerading as assertion.

Summary

In this chapter we have stepped back from assertive behaviour to look at the issue of rights. We have said that:
- Being clear on, and accepting, your rights and other people's rights enables you to know how others are behaving towards you, and helps you to behave assertively.
- The rights you accept are partly determined by the beliefs you hold, which in turn derive from the experiences you have.
- Accepting the responsibilities that go with your rights enables you to behave assertively as opposed to aggressively.

4. Starting to be more assertive

In preceding chapters we have dealt with some of the more theoretical aspects of assertiveness: the concepts themselves, recognizing assertive, aggressive and nonassertive behaviours, and your rights within assertiveness. In this chapter we begin the practical process of helping you to behave more assertively at work.

We believe that any skill, whether it be typewriting, public speaking, or interacting with others, can best be developed through practising. This is equally true of assertiveness. So, to start the practice we have chosen a number of situations that people have to handle at work. The situations are ones in which you might sometimes find yourself behaving aggressively or non-assertively. They occur fairly often, so there is usually plenty of opportunity to practise them. They are mostly short interactions with fairly straightforward outcomes, making them an ideal starting point for improving assertiveness. With each of the situations we give a number of hints for behaving assertively in them.

The situations we will be dealing with are: making requests, refusing requests, disagreeing and stating your views, giving praise, and receiving praise. For each of these situations we look at the beliefs people often hold (including the rights they think they have) which can lead to nonassertive or aggressive behaviour. We then give hints for behaving assertively in each of the situations.

Situation 1. Making requests

Do you sometimes find it difficult to make requests of other people at work, or are you very tentative or abrupt when doing so? Sometimes it is easier to make a request according to whom you are asking. So you might find it easier, say, to ask a colleague than to ask a member of staff or a superior. Typical requests might be: asking a colleague for a report earlier than usual, asking a manager for a change of responsibilities, asking a member of staff to work an extra weekend shift. If you are not able to make requests assertively, you can often end up missing opportunities, not taking initiatives, and not getting the best use out of available resources; alternatively, you might cause others to be resentful and uncooperative.

Any difficulties you might experience probably stem from the *beliefs* you hold about making requests. These may include:
– I'll put other people in a position where they can't refuse.
– If people refuse it means they don't like me.
– It's a sign of weakness to ask for things.
– My needs are not that important/not as important as other people's.

45

– If people do things for me it will put me under an obligation to them.

– I have no right to ask.

If you hold the above beliefs then it is likely that you will avoid making requests or you will make them apologetically. That is to say, you will act *nonassertively*.

In contrast, your beliefs may include:

– Others have no right to refuse.

– A refusal constitutes an attack upon me personally.

– My needs are more important than other people's.

– Other people ought to be pleased to help me out.

Then you will be hostile or demanding when making the request. The unspoken challenge indicated by your tone of voice is, 'Refuse if you dare!' With all of these you will be behaving *aggressively*.

It is realistic to expect that you will need to make requests of other people as part of your job. Some of these requests may well be for people to 'go beyond their call of duty'. We refer to both these as work requests. In addition, there will be times when you want to make other requests of someone, for example for a lift home, or to go for a drink at lunchtime. These we call personal requests. With all requests the key to behaving assertively is to believe that *you have the right to ask, the other person has the right to be asked in an assertive way, and the right to refuse*. With this last right there are sometimes exceptions, so that a person may not always have the right to refuse. For instance, in accepting a contract of employment for a particular job a person may have *relinquished* his right to refuse work at certain times or in certain circumstances. Even so, *he still has the right to state any problems that the request will cause*.

By the way, we make no distinctions between reasonable or unreasonable requests, largely because this can only be a subjective judgement anyway. Second, 'unreasonable' can be an emotive word, pushing you into responding with aggression. If you accept the assertive rights for both parties mentioned above, then the issue of reasonable versus unreasonable has less significance.

HINTS FOR MAKING REQUESTS

The aim is to make requests in a straightforward, open way; *not* to make it difficult for the other person to refuse.

Don't apologize profusely. For instance, 'I'm very sorry to bother you, I hope you don't mind. . .' or 'I hope you won't think I'm a nuisance, but do you think you could possibly. . .'

Be direct. For example, speaking to a colleague: 'Anne, I'd really like the report on the Harrison project by the end of next week. Can that be done?' If you make hints rather than requests people will either become suspicious or impatient or both, and say to themselves 'Why doesn't he get straight to the point?'

46

Keep it short. Long-winded explanations get confusing and increase the chances that you will start justifying yourself.

Don't justify yourself for making the request; e.g., 'I wouldn't normally ask anybody. I don't like to be a nuisance, but the car's broken down and the neighbour's in bed with flu.'

Give a reason for your request, if you think it will help, but be sure it's genuine and keep it brief. 'Pete, I shall be without the car tomorrow; would you be able to give me a lift?' or 'Alan, I need the figures for the meeting next week; will you be able to let me have yours by Friday?'

Don't 'sell' your request with flattery or tempting benefits: 'Linda, you're *just* the person, would you. . .' or 'Bob, I'm sure this will interest you, . . .'

Don't play on people's friendship or good nature: 'Be a pal and get this to me by dinner time' or 'It would be really kind of you if you could. . .'

Don't take a refusal personally, even when the request is of a more personal nature, or when the colleague is also a friend. Otherwise, he might end up feeling guilty about refusing.

Respect the other person's right to say no. With a personal request, take 'No' for an answer. Don't become persistent with nonassertive pleading or aggressive bullying. With a work request, give more information and clarification, find out why the person is unable to meet your request. If the answer is still 'No', put your energy into joint problem-solving rather than into necessarily persuading the other person to meet your request as originally outlined. (For further explanation of this see Chapter 11).

Situation 2. Refusing requests

A frequent experience for many managers and specialists is that, when faced with a request at work, they find it difficult to say 'No', or their 'No' comes across like a hammer blow. As with making requests, any difficulties you may have often stem from the *beliefs* you hold. These could include things like:
– Others will feel angry/hurt if I refuse.
– They'll cease to like me.
– It's rude/selfish to refuse.
– I have no right to refuse.
– If I refuse, I relinquish the right to make requests of others.
– Their needs are more important than mine.
These beliefs will lead you to say 'Yes' when you really want to say 'No', to feel guilty about saying 'No', or to give excuses (instead of the real reason) for not agreeing to the request. An example of this last one would be saying: 'I can't take on the survey at the moment, I haven't got time', when the real reason is you do not think the survey is of value. All of this is behaving *nonassertively*.

Later on, after having said 'Yes' when you really wanted to say No', you might find you have taken on more work than you can handle. You can also

47

start to feel resentful that you, or others, are doing things you are far from happy about. You may even take this resentment out on the person who made the request, whereas in fact you are angry at yourself for not saying 'No'.

In contrast to the above beliefs, you might *believe* that:
– Others have no right to make such requests of you.
– Other people ought to sort themselves out.
– If I meet their requests people will soon get the idea I'm a 'soft touch'.
These beliefs will result in responses like 'Not likely, you've got a nerve' or, 'Why ask me all the time?' which are examples of *aggressively* refusing a request.

The key to refusing requests assertively is to believe that *other people have the right to ask; you have the right to refuse.* Where the definition of the job limits your right to refuse, remember *you still have the right to state the difficulties the request will cause.*

HINTS FOR REFUSING REQUESTS ASSERTIVELY

Keep the reply short, avoiding long rambling justifications along the lines of: 'I wouldn't normally say no, only . . . you know how it is, I hope you don't mind.'

Simply say: 'No, I don't want to . . .' or 'I prefer not to . . .' or 'I'd rather not . . .' or 'I'm not happy to . . .' These phrases are particularly useful for refusing personal requests.

Give a reason for refusing if you want to, but do not invent an excuse.

Avoid 'I can't' phrases because they easily start sounding like excuses.

Don't apologize profusely: 'I'm terribly sorry . . . do you mind very much if . . .'

Acknowledge the requester when she has invited you to do something or when she has taken an unusual initiative for her: 'Thank you, Anne, but I'm not ready to take my coffee break yet', or 'I'm certainly interested in the meetings, Pat, but . . .'

Honestly state limitations/possibilities: 'I won't be able to . . .'; 'No, it will be difficult/impossible to . . . but I will . . .'. These are particularly useful with requests about work!

Ask for clarification or more information, such as 'What detail does the survey need to go into?' 'Do you need it by Friday morning or later in the afternoon?'

Ask for more time to decide on the request, for instance if you want to check workloads.

Nonverbal behaviour. Especially with short replies you need to slow down, speak steadily and with warmth, otherwise replies like 'No, I don't want to' can sound abrupt.

48

IF THE REQUESTER BECOMES PERSISTENT

Often people ignore your right to refuse, and they become persistent in making their request. We are not so much thinking of people asking for more information or clarification when you refuse, but of people using ploys like the following to get you to change your mind:

– Questioning your judgement: 'Are you sure about that?'
– Non assertive pleading: 'It wouldn't half, um. . . get me out of a hole if you. . . .'
– Aggressive (sometimes 'fatherly') bullying: 'Oh go on. I'm sure you can!'
– Blaming you: 'You'll leave me with a terrible problem.'

When people become persistent we suggest the following:

Repeat your refusal, adding the reason if you didn't give it first time. Leave out the reason if you did give it. Slow down and emphasize any words you are repeating.

Don't search for 'better' reasons. You will probably only come up with flimsy excuses that the requester will either propose 'solutions' to or dismiss altogether. This example demonstrates what can often happen:

Initial assertive refusal	'I don't think Steve is the best person to do the annual schedule.'
Persistence	'It wouldn't take long to train him.'
Excuse	'I haven't got time.'
Persistence	'Dave could train him for you.'
Excuse	'Besides, Steve is working on the invoice system.'
Persistence	'That can easily wait till afterwards.'

As soon as you put forward excuses you are becoming dishonest and making life difficult for yourself. So after the first persistent statement it would have been more honest and more productive to say something like: 'No, *I prefer* Steve to work on the invoice system.' If you inadvertently give an excuse, then retrieve the situation by 'coming clean' with the real reason as soon as you can.

Situation 3. Disagreeing and stating your views

At work and in your social life you experience different events from other people; even with the same event you might experience it in different ways. All this leads you, quite legitimately, to see things from your own point of view. This will sometimes be the same as other people's, sometimes different. You probably exchange these points of view when you meet with colleagues, subordinates, or superiors. This either can be in casual encounters, where viewpoints are aired more or less as an end in themselves or it can be in more formal meetings, where disagreeing and stating views is part of the larger processes of decision making and problem solving. Unfortunately, both casual encounters and more formal meetings at times resemble a 'battle of wits', with enormous energy going into 'point scoring', rather like a debating society; or else they adopt a cocktail party atmosphere, where the game is to change your mind as soon as anybody disagrees with you. The following exchange illustrates both point scoring and changing your mind.

The situation is that a new system for budget returns has been in trial operation for a month. This is being reviewed in a meeting:

DAVE: 'I reckon the new procedure's a real improvement.
   The old one never worked properly.'
COLIN: 'That's not true. The old one was far better. This
   new one takes too long to fill in, for a start. It wants
   scrapping altogether.'
LIZ: 'It's all right if you know what you're doing.'   (*Point scoring*)
COLIN: 'On the contrary, it's all right if you've got plenty   (*Point scoring*)
   of time to spare.'
DAVE: 'Well, I suppose it is a bit time consuming in some   (*Change of mind*)
   ways.'

In this exchange there is no attempt to recognize each other's position. In fact, all the points of view are valid, in that, while the new system may not work for Colin, it may well work for Liz and Dave. The likely outcome of the exchange is that, whatever system is adopted, it will meet the needs of one, maybe two, people but not all. A more useful outcome would be a system that meets the needs of all parties. But to achieve that kind of outcome the behaviour would need to be assertive, instead of as it was—mainly aggressive, with some nonassertion.

So, *aggressive behaviour* often stokes up conflict by emphasizing disagreement and down-playing agreement. It tends to dismiss the other person's ideas and opinions as worthless, to state opinions as facts, and to take up an entrenched position. It puts down the other person either through sarcasm or direct hostility. It uses statements like:
– 'Nonsense, that won't work.'
– 'You don't know what you're talking about.'
– 'That will just cause problems.'
– 'That machine is a complete waste of time.'
– 'Another of your time-saving ideas, would you say?'
– I don't care what you say, I'm sticking to . . .'
   Aggressive behaviour stems from *beliefs* along the lines of:
– Things are always black and white; there are no grey areas.
– Other people can only be right if I'm wrong: both parties can't be right.
– I'm more vulnerable if I'm seen to be wrong.
– It will show weakness if I change my mind.
– Other people have no right to disagree with me.

50

The immediate result of people disagreeing and stating their views *aggressively* is that the issues can get forgotten as the emotions start to take over. Thus, new facts, valid viewpoints, and potentially useful ideas get lost. In turn, this means that the eventual outcomes, such as solutions and decisions, are not as effective as they could be.

Nonassertive behaviour dismisses your own ideas and opinions as being worthless or less important than those of other people. It seeks to avoid open conflict by glossing over any disagreements that exist and by changing tack in the face of other people's challenges. It expresses disagreement and viewpoints tentatively or apologetically, if at all. It may sometimes involve keeping quiet about doubts altogether or airing them afterwards to different people. It consists of statements like:
- 'Mmm, I suppose you're right, . . . really.'
- 'Er, . . . I'm not sure I can agree there.'
- 'I don't like to disagree but, . . . um, . . . have you. . .?'
- 'Oh, . . . really? . . . well . . . maybe I've got the wrong impression.'
It arises out of *beliefs* that include:
- Disagreeing always leads to conflict, which is unpleasant.
- People will think I'm just being awkward if I raise doubts.
- Other people will always be upset or annoyed if I disagree.
- If I state my point of view I stand the risk of being wrong/ridiculed, etc.
- Both parties can't be right.
- I'm usually wrong anyway.
- I don't have the right to disagree.
The immediate result of being nonassertive about disagreeing and stating views is that some quite valid difficulties are not raised and are therefore not taken into account in any eventual solutions. Also, decisions can be taken to which you are not fully committed. Other people will be understandably irritated when you admit later on: 'Well, I didn't really agree with it at the time but I didn't like to say so.'

Assertive behaviour involves disagreeing and agreeing openly and stating your viewpoints clearly and firmly. It means that you do not put yourself or others down. It comes from *beliefs* such as:
- I and others have the right to have opinions and for these to be different.
- I and others have the right to state opinions and to disagree.
- Disagreements do not necessarily lead to conflict.
- Opinions are not necessarily right and wrong, merely different.

HINTS FOR DISAGREEING AND STATING YOUR VIEWS ASSERTIVELY
State disagreement clearly: 'No, I disagree with . . .'; 'No, I don't go along with . . .'.
Express doubts in a constructive way: 'Will that lead to X?' or 'I see a

51

difficulty in that . . . . Can we get round it?' rather than knocking people's ideas down like skittles: 'That won't work' or 'That will cause Y'.

Use 'I' statements to distinguish your opinion from fact and to distinguish your experience from that of other people:
- 'As I see it, . . .';
- 'I believe . . .';
- 'I find that . . .';
- 'My experience is . . .'.

Change your opinion in the light of new information (rather than as a result of emotional behaviour from other people) and be firm and honest about doing so: 'In the light of . . . I now think. . .'.

Give reasons for your disagreement if you think it will lead to more progress. 'I don't agree with X because of the effect it has on Y.'

State what parts you agree and disagree with: 'I don't agree that the procedure affects *all* departments in that way' or 'I agree that we need to change, but not as quickly as you suggest.'

Recognize other people's point of view. 'I appreciate that you see it differently from me'; 'I recognize that it affects you differently'.

The result of disagreeing and stating your views assertively is that information, viewpoints, and ideas do not get lost; issues are not avoided or 'fudged'. It increases the chances that further down the track people will be able to come up with mutually acceptable solutions.

Situation 4. Giving praise

We often hear managers say things like 'You only hear from Dave when something goes wrong'. It is quite common for people to be working in an environment where praise is nonexistent, or where the recipient of the rare morsel thinks suspiciously, 'What's he after now?' There are a number of reasons why you might not give praise, including your *beliefs* about giving praise, such as:
- It's soft or soggy to give praise.
- If I praise them they'll start relaxing (the standards).
- They're only doing what they're paid for.
- They'll think I want something.
- People will only learn to do better if you point out their mistakes, so praise doesn't serve any useful purpose.

In addition, you might be reluctant to give praise because your *experiences* of giving praise in the past have been unrewarding; maybe:
- You felt uncomfortable or embarrassed.
- You couldn't find the right words.
- The praise turned 'sour' on you.
- It was not well received.

52

All this means that now you might behave *nonassertively*, and either avoid giving praise altogether, or else give praise:

– Apologetically: 'I hope you won't mind my saying so, but I really thought you handled that customer well.'
– Hesitantly, so it comes across less sincerely: 'Sylvia, I liked . . . er, I mean I thought your report was really very good.'
– And at the same time put yourself down; 'Pat, I thought your presentation was good. I wish mine were as good as that.'

Alternatively, you might behave *aggressively*, in that you give the praise:

– Grudgingly: 'Well, that wasn't a bad effort for you, Jim'; or 'You did it well, in the end.' Here you are giving and taking back at the same time.
– With double meaning: 'That was an interesting presentation, John. Did Sue help you prepare it?' The intention is to praise, but the implication is that John couldn't have produced it on his own.
– Gushingly: 'That was absolutely splendid, Jones. I thought you did a really magnificent job. Well done! Keep up the good work.' So either the praise comes over as insincere or you end up patronizing the other person—treating him as a father might treat a child.

Notes

1. Sometimes people use sarcasm: 'That was really *some* report.' This is usually not praise but criticism disguised as praise.
2. You might make some of the above statements as a joke; e.g., 'You did it well in the end!' If you know the person well then they will take the joke in good part, knowing that at the same time you are sincere about the underlying praise.

If you are unable to give praise assertively you leave people trying to guess whether the work they do meets your expectations, or making assumptions along the lines of 'no news is good news'.

Assertive behaviour involves expressing thoughts, feelings, beliefs and wants in direct, honest and appropriate ways. Because of the interchange of ideas and resources that occurs between people at work, it is inevitable that there will be times when you want to acknowledge someone for what she has done or said. This person may be a colleague, a member of staff, or a senior manager; or even a client or supplier. In addition to showing acknowledgement, praise also has a *learning function*. People learn not only from mistakes but also from successes. So praise, especially very specific praise, gives the other person a picture of your standards and informs her when she has achieved them.

HINTS FOR GIVING PRAISE

Maintain eye contact, but in a relaxed way: not looking away as though embarrassed to give praise, but not staring the person down.

Keep the praise brief and clear, avoiding extra phrases to pad it out and make it more 'comfortable'.

Use 'I' statements along the lines of 'I like the report on . . .'; 'I'm pleased with the way you handled the visit, Dave.'

Make it specific to detailed aspects of the work wherever possible. 'I liked the report on . . . I think it was a good idea to have the summary at the beginning because it makes it easier for the reader. . . .'

Statements like the last one are *analysing the successes in terms of the effect they have*. This gives people information about what would be useful to repeat in future and *why*.

Situation 5. Receiving praise

All too often you might feel uncomfortable or foolish when you are on the receiving end of praise. This is often because, from your culture or upbringing, you have come to hold certain *beliefs* about receiving praise. For instance:
– It's impolite/boastful to agree with praise.
– Accepting praise means being obligated/grateful to someone.
So you fall into one of the following traps:

Behaving nonassertively
– Shrugging off the praise: 'Oh, it was nothing, really it wasn't.'
– Giving praise in return: 'Er, I think your last report was good as well.'
– Putting yourself down: 'Well, I'm not really very good. Keith's brilliant at organizing these studies.'

Behaving aggressively
– Challenging the person's judgement: 'You thought that was good? I thought it was second rate, myself.'
– Putting the other person down: 'Yes, it was a jolly sight better than your last effort.'
– Boastfulness: 'Well, of course it was. I always make a good presentation.'
Both the nonassertive and the aggressive responses above discount the praise. They thus reduce the chances that the giver will want to repeat the exercise.

HINTS FOR RECEIVING PRAISE ASSERTIVELY
Keep your response short: 'Thanks, Dave, I'm glad you liked it.'
Simply thank the giver: 'Thanks, Dave.'
Agree with or accept the praise: 'Thanks, Liz, I thought the presentation went well'; or 'Thank you, Liz, I was pleased with the way it went'. If you also like something it is assertive to say so.

Note

If you disagree with the praise, certainly qualify your reply but still thank the giver: 'Thank you Sue . . . although I didn't feel too pleased with it myself.'

Conclusion

The five situations we have dealt with provide a useful starting point in behaving more assertively, as they do not usually require long or complex assertions. However, handling them more successfully can give a big return for the time invested.

In Chapter 7 we will look at the other side of the coin to 'giving and receiving praise', which is 'giving and receiving criticism'. This is more complicated and is best dealt with after reading the next two chapters.

5. Types of assertion

We have talked so far of three types of behaviour: ass, agg, and n.a. Already you may have realized that these are umbrella categories, covering a range of behaviours. So there are different types of assertion, just as there are different types of n.a. and agg. In this chapter we introduce six different types of assertion and give some guidelines on when and how to use them. At the end of the chapter, there is a short recognition test to help you identify the different types.

We suggest you regard these types as some of the options you have available within the spectrum of assertiveness. Some of them you will use already, perhaps in a slightly different format. Being able to use all the types gives you a greater repertoire of behaviours for handling the wide range of situations you encounter. In future chapters (such as Chapter 9, 'Handling Aggression from Others') we will build these types into strategies for dealing with specific situations.

Six types of assertion

There are several types of assertion, but the ones we find useful are

Basic	Negative feelings
Empathetic	Consequence
Discrepancy	Responsive

We will go on to give definitions and examples for each of these types, so that you can distinguish them.

BASIC ASSERTION

This is a straightforward statement where you stand up for your rights. It involves making clear your needs, wants, beliefs, opinions, or feelings. Examples of basic assertion are:
– 'As I see it, the system is working well.'
– 'The presentation starts at 9 a.m. in the board room.'
– 'I need to be away by 5 o'clock.'
– The cost is £2000.'
– 'I feel very pleased with the way the issue has been resolved.'

When to use basic assertion

This is the most common form of assertion, which you use everyday to make your needs, wants, and opinions known. In addition, you use it to give praise or compliments, information, and facts to others. It is particularly appropriate to use it when you are raising an issue with someone for the first time. So, for instance, it would be the starting point for your discussion with your manager over a regrading of your job. You might say: 'Doug, I'd like to talk about regrading my job. Now as I see it, (state the position) . . . . So what I'd like to happen is . . . (state your suggestion).' All these are basic assertions.

You can also repeat a basic assertion to re-emphasize your needs and wants, when you feel that your initial statement of them is being ignored or played down.

EMPATHETIC ASSERTION

This assertion contains the element of empathy as well as a statement of your needs or wants. By empathy we mean the ability to put yourself in the other person's position and recognize the feelings, needs, and wants that he may have. Some examples of empathetic assertion are:
– 'I appreciate that you don't like the new procedure. However, until it's changed I'd like you to keep your people working to it.'
– 'I know you're busy at the moment, John, but I'd like to make a quick request of you.'
– 'I recognize that it's difficult to be precise on costs at this stage, but it would be helpful if you'd give me a rough estimate.'
As you see from these examples, empathy is different from sympathy, although the two are sometimes confused. Sympathy usually involves feeling sorry for someone, and leaves people where they are—feeling sorry for themselves. This works against your behaving assertively towards them. For instance: 'What a shame you didn't get that job. I know you must be feeling very disappointed. Ah well . . . there we are.' By contrast, empathy gives due recognition for where people are, and also moves them or you forward: 'I recognize that you're very disappointed about not getting that job . . . . I think there will be other opportunities.'

When to use empathetic assertion
Empathetic assertion can be used when the other person is engrossed in a situation and you want to indicate that you are aware of and sensitive to his situation. So acknowledging that someone is busy, has a different opinion than you, or feels particularly strongly about an issue shows that you recognize his position. This enables the other person to realize that you are not dismissing him, which in turn increases the chances that he will recognize your position and respond assertively. Empathy is an essential ingredient for resolving conflicts in which people are behaving aggressively. (We refer to this in Chapter 9.)

Empathetic assertion is also useful in holding you back from over-reacting with aggression. This is roughly how it works. With empathy you have to give yourself time to imagine the other person's position, so automatically you

57

slow down your response to him. When this happens you are less likely to see him as an aggressive person who is personally stopping your needs from being met. You can then go on and behave assertively towards him.

Empathetic assertion can be powerful behaviour, so it is important not to use it as a means of getting your own needs met at the expense of the other person's. It is easy to over-use phrases like 'I appreciate your feelings on this, but . . .' so that the currency of empathy is debased. Just ritually repeating these phrases is really aggression masked as assertion, because you would not really be taking the other person's views or feelings into account.

Sometimes, 'putting yourself in the other person's position' could lead you to behave nonassertively. So, for instance, if you see that a colleague is busy, you might say to yourself, 'Oh it wouldn't be fair to ask Bob to help out', and as a result would not even ask him. In this case you are denying your right to ask and his right to say no; you are taking a decision for the other person. Your empathy is spilling over into sympathy.

DISCREPANCY ASSERTION

By this we mean pointing out the discrepancy between what has previously been agreed and what is actually happening or about to happen. It often concludes with a statement of your needs and wants. So for instance:

– 'As I understood it, we agreed that project A was top priority. Now you're asking me to give more time to project B. I'd like to clarify which is now the priority.'
– 'Mike, I remember in my recent appraisal you said you would delegate more of the correspondence work to me. I'm still keen to do that.'

When to use discrepancy assertion

It is useful to regard discrepancy assertion as a *starting point* for when you suspect that there is a contradiction in what has been agreed and what is happening, or about to happen. It helps you to establish whether there is an actual contradiction, or whether there was simply a misunderstanding of the agreement between you and the other person. If there is a misunderstanding you can then clarify the issue and make a new agreement. If, on the other hand, there is a contradiction, you can go on and discover the reason for this, before taking further action. Thus, if the other person had merely forgotten the original agreement then your discrepancy assertion is usually sufficient to restore the status quo. On the other hand, if the person has chosen to ignore the previous agreement, then your discrepancy assertion makes it clear that you recall the agreement and wish it to stand. At the same time, it gives him the opportunity to revert back to the original agreement. Or it brings out in the open the fact that he no longer feels bound by it. From here you can find out whether circumstances have changed to make the previous agreement impractical. If not, then you could use a basic assertion to restate that you would like the agreement to stand.

Discrepancy assertion can also be used when there is contradiction between a person's *present* words and deeds. For example, a colleague who says, 'I really think we could improve cooperation between your department and ours' and then launches into a lengthy attack on your staff: 'The trouble with your department is you've got too many people who think they know it all. They'll never . . . . They don't . . . . I can't ever see . . . (etc.).' A discrepancy assertion will point out how this inconsistent behaviour is working against what he wants. 'Hang on, Paul, on the one hand you are wanting to improve cooperation between our departments, but on the other hand you are making statements that make it difficult for us to cooperate. I agree with you that we *can* improve cooperation, so I'd like to take a look at that.' This also encourages the person to decide what he really wants.

NEGATIVE FEELINGS ASSERTION
Here you are making a statement that draws the attention of another person to the undesirable effect his behaviour is having on you. So it can contain the following four elements, not necessarily in the order given:

1. When . . .   (an objective description of other's behaviour).
2. The effects are . . .   (how that behaviour specifically affects you).
3. I feel . . .   (a description of your feelings).
4. I'd like . . .   (a statement of what you want or prefer).

An example is:
'*When* you let me have your return at this late stage,
it involves my working over the weekend.
I feel annoyed about this,
so in future *I'd like* to have it by Friday lunchtime.'

When to use negative feelings assertion
You can use this when the other person is still ignoring your rights in spite of your having raised an issue several times on previous occasions. Or you can use it when the person is repeatedly violating your rights during a single interaction. At this point you would be likely to experience very strong negative feelings—anger, resentment, hurt, and the like—and the advantage of negative feelings assertion is that it gives you a mechanism for expressing these feelings openly, without making an uncontrolled emotional outburst, and without denying these feelings exist. (For more guidance on handling negative feelings, see also Chapter 6.) So negative feelings assertion enables you to take responsibility for your feelings and to express them assertively. In a later section we look at *how* to use this behaviour.

In addition, negative feelings assertion is very powerful in alerting the other

59

person to the effects of his action on you—even without the 'I feel . . .' part. You may not wish to talk of your feelings in some situations (for instance, with certain people or within certain organizational climates). In this case we suggest you omit the 'I feel' part, emphasize instead the 'when' and 'the effects' parts—without actually *blaming* the other person—and then state what you would like. In many cases this will be sufficient for the other person to agree to changes. In other cases the negative feelings assertion may be only a first step because it uncovers an underlying problem between you. Thus, in the above example it may be that the late return resulted from an unrealistic workload. This then becomes the problem you need to resolve.

CONSEQUENCE ASSERTION

This informs the other person of the future consequences for him of *not* changing his behaviour. It also includes an opportunity to change that behaviour before the consequences occur. So, for instance:
– 'If you continue to withhold the information, I'm left with no option but to bring in the production director. I'd prefer not to.'
– 'I'm not prepared, John, to let any of my staff cooperate with yours on the project, unless you give them access to the same facilities that your people have.'
– 'If this occurs again I'm left with no alternative but to apply the formal disciplinary procedure. I'd prefer not to.'

When to use consequence assertion
As it is the strongest form of assertion, we see consequence assertion as a last-resort behaviour, to be used sparingly and only when the other types have failed. It is easy for consequence behaviour to be seen as threatening and thus aggressive. Some hints on how to reduce the chances of this happening are given later in this chapter.

You can use consequence assertion only when you have sanctions to apply. These might be: referring an issue to a higher level of management, giving a request a lower level of priority than usual, reducing a budget, limiting your cooperation, or applying a recognized disciplinary procedure. In addition, you can use consequence assertion only when you are *prepared* to apply the sanctions. Otherwise you would lose credibility. Even when you have sanctions and are prepared to use them, there is the question: 'What sanctions does the other person have to use in return?'

In the light of all this you might decide not to use a consequence assertion. Then, the alternative is a negative feelings assertion, which emphasizes the 'I feel' part of the behaviour.

RESPONSIVE ASSERTION
We have listed this one last, not because it is least important, but because it is a

60

rather different animal. The emphasis with this behaviour is upon *finding out where other people stand*—their needs, wants, opinions, feelings. This is often achieved by asking questions, but can also be done by statements making it clear that you would like to hear from them. Examples of both forms are:
– 'What are your reservations about the new approach?'
– 'How long can you give me to try and persuade him?'
– 'What problems does that create for you?'
– 'What would you prefer to do?'
– 'John, I'd like to hear your views on this one.'
– 'I'd like you to say which approach is better from your department's point of view.'

When to use responsive assertion
Responsive assertion is the *vehicle* for checking out that, in standing up for you own rights, you are not violating the rights of others. You would use it when the other person has behaved nonassertively—not speaking up at all, or doing so only indirectly—to find out what his needs, wants, opinions, etc., are. You would also use it, regardless of whether people have behaved aggressively, nonassertively, or assertively, when you want to know whether a particular course of action is acceptable to them. In addition, you would use responsive assertion when you want to collect information from people; for instance, 'Dave, what is the deadline for that project?' You would use it when you suspect there is a misunderstanding between you that could create difficulties. So you would check out your understanding of what the other person is saying, or find out his understanding of something.

So responsive assertion can be used on its own like this, or it can be used in conjunction with other types of assertion, especially basic, empathetic, and discrepancy. So statements like 'I'd like to take the overtime item first; how does that fit in with you?' not only make your preference clear, but also encourage the other person to say if this approach meets his needs. The responsive part of the statement has two effects. First, it increases the chances that your behaviour will be seen as assertive rather than aggressive. Following on from this, it increases the likelihood of the other person's responding assertively to this perceived assertion. This is particularly so when dealing with people who tend towards nonassertion. Responsive assertion, therefore, paves the way for interactions to become assertive/assertive exchanges. This is crucial to assertiveness if both parties' needs are to be met and conflicts resolved (see Chapter 12).

We have described six types of assertion, together with examples of each. This information is summarized for easy reference in Table 5.1 at the end of the chapter. We have so far said specifically when you might use each of the different types. In the next section we make some general notes on using all these types of assertion.

61

When to use different assertions—general notes

As a guiding principle for deciding what type of assertiveness to use, we say: *use the minimum degree of assertion for achieving your aim*. For most situations this usually involves starting with lower levels and moving up to higher levels. So does this mean the types can be arranged into a strict hierarchy according to their strength? Not really, though you would probably agree with us that consequence is stronger than empathetic assertion. That apart, for convenience we usually divide the assertions into two levels:
– Lower level: basic, responsive, empathetic
– Higher level: discrepancy, negative feelings, consequence
Even so, this is a rough and ready distinction because the perceived strength of the behaviour will depend, among other things, on the words used and on the nonverbal behaviour. However, let us demonstrate the 'minimum degree' principle with the example of Jenny taking an item back to a shop. Her aim was to get the faulty item replaced with a good one.

JENNY: 'I bought this alarm clock here yesterday. The *(Basic)*
button for moving the hands isn't working properly
so I'd like to exchange it.'

The assistant could have agreed to exchange the clock,
or he could have 'hassled' by saying something like:

ASSISTANT: 'The clock should have been checked before
it left the shop.'

Then Jenny could have replied:

JENNY: 'I realize that would have made things easier; *(Empathetic)*
however, I would still like it replaced.'
or *or*
'I would still like it replaced.' *(Basic)*

At this point the assistant may agree but may not. So
after several exchanges Jenny would raise the level of
assertion:

JENNY: 'I would like the item changed. If you are not *(Consequence)*
prepared to do that I will take the matter to your
Head Office. I would prefer to resolve it now.'

You might be wondering: 'Why not wade in straightaway with a consequence assertion—it would save a lot of time.' Unfortunately, we cannot prove or disprove this particular claim. But one of the snags with using a consequence or any of the higher levels of assertion too early in a situation is that you leave yourself with fewer options and thus less room for manoeuvre. After all, once

62

you have stated a consequence, if the other person still ignores your rights then you either climb down or carry out the sanction! The danger is that you get locked into applying the sanctions against your better judgement.

Another snag with the 'shoot first, ask later' theory is that you never know whether your victim was innocent! So in the example of the shop assistant you would never know whether he *might* have agreed in response to a lower-level assertion. We are amazed how many of the tricky situations that *we* face can be resolved successfully with lower levels of assertion. But this is something for you to test out! Besides, you have nothing to lose—you can more easily move up the scale than down.

Undoubtedly, if you use a strong assertion early in a situation the other person will more likely perceive this as aggression. When this happens (unless she has learned to handle you assertively!) she responds with either aggression or nonassertion; whereas the aim in using the types of assertion is to get assertive–assertive exchanges, because the outcomes of these exchanges on the whole are more satisfactory to both parties.

Now that you are more familiar with the different types of assertion, you may have a concern about whether you would be seen as assertive in using some of them (for example, consequence or discrepancy). It will help enormously if you follow the 'minimum degree' principle. However, it is also crucial that your nonverbal behaviours and the actual words you use are clearly assertive. The next section aims to help you in these two areas.

How to say the types of assertion—assertively

It is quite possible to be seen as nonassertive or aggressive when using the six behaviours described above. It may be the actual words you use, or the nonverbal behaviours that accompany them. The rest of this section is intended to complement and take further the verbal and nonverbal characteristics of ass, agg, and n.a. described in Chapter 2. We will look at the six types in turn.

BASIC ASSERTION

The only new point we wish to make here concerns repeating a basic assertion in order to re-emphasize your needs and wants. For your assertion to be seen as *stronger*, you can make it shorter than your initial statement, saying each word slower and louder than before, and giving more or less equal weight to each word: 'I . would . like . it . replaced.' Or you can make the repeat statements the same length as before, but giving more emphasis to the key words: 'I would *still* like to have it *replaced* with a *new* one.'

EMPATHETIC ASSERTION

We mentioned earlier that the important thing here is to avoid 'ritual' use of this behaviour. You can achieve this by slowing down and giving emphasis to the 'I understand/appreciate' part of the behaviour. The tone of voice needs to be warm and sincere rather than having a hint of exasperation or irritation in it. Good eye contact also helps to convey sincerity.

DISCREPANCY ASSERTION

When using this behaviour it is important to describe the discrepancy in a 'matter of fact' way; otherwise it comes across as accusing the other person of breaking an agreement. ('You *said* you were going to get that done by the end of last week': the spoken or unspoken message is '. . . and it's your fault it hasn't been done.' This may be a risky assumption.) Making your statement in a matter of fact way means keeping your voice at a constant pace and not letting the pitch rise up at the end. Prefacing your statement with phrases that emphasize *your* interpretation of the agreement ('as I understood it'; 'the way I remember it') help to uncover misunderstandings at an early stage in the interaction.

NEGATIVE FEELINGS ASSERTION

These statements also can easily be seen as accusing and blaming. Saying them in a matter of fact way is again important. In addition, there are two other things you can do. One is to make your statement in the form of: 'When you do X, it leads to Y; I feel Z'—as opposed to: 'When you do X, it leads to Y; you make me feel Z'. This may seem a small distinction, but there is a dramatic difference in the meaning and effect of these two. In the second you are blaming the other person for making you feel the way you do—which is likely to bring forth an aggressive 'That's your problem' type reply, or a nonassertive apology. In the first version *you* are retaining responsibility for how you feel—which is more likely to lead to an assertive response: 'I wasn't aware of that' or 'that isn't what I intended'. We discuss the issue of responsibility for feelings in Chapter 6.

Second, be specific when you describe both the other person's behaviour and the concrete effects. So, for example:
– 'When you continually knock down other people's suggestions in our department meetings, it makes it difficult for us to reach agreement'
as opposed to:
– 'When you behave so negatively in our department meetings it really does make life difficult for me'
The more generalized the description of that person's behaviour, the more difficult it is for him to see the link between his behaviour and its effects. In turn, the more likely he is to take it as a personal attack and thus respond aggressively.

CONSEQUENCE ASSERTION

This type of assertion presents particular difficulties for many people because it is the strongest form of assertion. It is closest to aggression and so it can

64

easily be seen as a threat. To avoid this, keep the words themselves factual, rather than emotional and personal. For example, 'If you do X, I will have no option but to do Y' is not a *personal* attack upon the other person, but a factual statement of what will happen. Again, describe 'X' and 'Y' in specific rather than generalized terms, avoiding statements like 'If you keep undermining my position, I'll have to retaliate'. Even where the words you use are assertive, you can be seen as threatening because of the accompanying nonverbal elements, Try saying the following consequence assertion out loud in different ways:

'If you continue to withold the information, I'm left with no option but to bring in the production director. I'd prefer not to.'

Did you:

– Say it very quickly, voice rising towards 'the production director' bit?
– Drive home your meaning, say, by pointing your finger on the 'if you' part?
– Glare or slant your eyes at some imaginary person?
– Move your head or your body forward?

Then you would be likely to be seen as threatening or menacing. So, to give the information in a neutral way:

– Hold your voice at medium volume with steady pace and pitch.
– Emphasize key words like verbs and nouns ('withhold', 'information', 'option', etc.) rather than pronouns ('you', 'me').
– Slow down the last sentence.
– Keep your eye contact firm but not glaring and your head upright.

We find also that phrases like 'I'd prefer not to', or 'I'd like to resolve this between ourselves' give the other person an opportunity to consider the consequences you have mentioned and decide whether, in the light of them, he wishes to modify his behaviour in any way.

RESPONSIVE ASSERTION

Although a very different behaviour from consequence assertion, this can also be seen as threatening, as though the other person is being interrogated. The following question is intended to collect 'neutral' information:

'Peter, how long did you say it will take you to finish that report?'

Try saying it in various ways. It is possible to make it sound incredulous, or as if you are accusing him of lying, or as though you do not trust his judgement—all by different emphases, and inflections in the voice.

To avoid this we have found it useful to practise saying to yourself easy, 'seeking information'-type questions followed by more difficult questions— *both in the same tone of voice.* For instance 'Peter, what is the mileage to Manchester?' followed by 'Peter, what happened on your visit last week?'

Summary

By way of summary for this chapter, Table 5.1 pulls together into a convenient

65

format the different types of assertion, with definition and examples of each.

In order to test your own understanding of the different types, we suggest you work through the recognition exercise in Table 5.2. You will probably find Table 5.1 a useful prompt for working through the exercise.

Table 5.1. Summary of types of assertion

Type	Definition	Examples
Basic	A straightforward statement that stands up for your rights by making clear your needs, wants, beliefs, opinions or feelings	'As I see it the system is working well.' 'I need to be away by 17.00 hours.' 'I feel very pleased with the way the issue has been resolved.'
Empathetic	A behaviour that contains an element of empathy as well as a statement of your needs and wants	'I appreciate that you don't like the new procedure. However, until it's changed I'd like you to keep your people working to it.' 'I know you're busy at the moment, John, but I'd like to make a quick request of you.'
Discrepancy	A statement that points out the difference between what has previously been agreed, and what is actually happening or about to happen	'As I understood it, we agreed that project A was top priority. Now you're asking me to give more time to project B. I'd like to clarify which is now priority.'
Negative feelings	A statement that draws the attention of another person to the undesirable effect that his behaviour is having on you. It can contain the following elements: – When . . . – The effects are . . . – I feel . . . – I'd like . . .	'*When* you let me have your return at this late stage, it involves me working over the weekend. *I feel* annoyed about this. *I'd like* in future to have it by Friday lunchtime.'
Consequence	A statement that informs the other person of the consequences for him of *not* changing his behaviour. It also gives him an opportunity to change that behaviour	'I'm not prepared, John, to let any of my staff cooperate with yours on the project unless you give them access to the same facilities that your people have.' 'If this occurs again, I'm left with no alternative but to apply the formal disciplinary procedure. I'd prefer not to.'

Table 5.1 *(continued)*

Type	Definition	Examples
Responsive	A behaviour that aims to find out where the other person stands, his needs, wants, opinions, and feelings	'What problems does that create for you?' 'What would you prefer to do?' 'John, I'd like to hear your views on this one.'

Table 5.2. Recognition exercise: Types of assertion

The following exercise contains 25 examples of assertive behaviours. You are asked to state what type of assertion each example is. The exercise is not intended as a test of memory, so please use Table 5.1 as an aid.

On each page there is space for you to write your answer in the *right*-hand column. Our suggested answer for each behaviour is given on the *line below* in the *left*-hand column. This will enable you to check your own answer before moving on to the next example.

Start by covering up all the answers on the left-hand side, and then reveal them, one at a time, to check your answers against ours.

At the end of the exercise, we suggest you look back to any examples where your answer differed from ours, and see if there is a particular type of assertion that is causing difficulty. If there is, we suggest you refer back to the text for the original definition and examples.

If you agree with 20 or more of the suggested answers, that is fine at this stage.

Suggested answer	Example	Your answer
↓	1. 'What ideas do you have for improving the existing methods?'	
Responsive	2. 'There are about 15 people involved.'	
Basic	3. 'I haven't thought about that before. I'd like time to think about your idea.'	
Basic	4. 'When you continually interrupt me while I'm working on the balance sheets, it means I have to start all over again. I'm feeling irritated by this, so I'd prefer you to wait till I finish a sheet.'	
Negative feelings	5. 'I thought we said we'd limit the scope of the research, but now you're talking of further developments. I'd rather stick with our plan, and keep the developments till later.'	

Table 5.2 (*continued*)

Suggested answer	Example	Your answer
Discrepancy	6. 'How do you think that will work out? Will there be any problems?'	
Responsive	7. 'I'd like you to take this request seriously; otherwise we'll discuss it with the department head. I'd prefer not to.'	
Consequence	8. 'Dave, I recognize that you're wanting to chat for a while, but I don't want to spend any more time now. I'd like to get on with the letters.'	
Empathetic	9. 'I'm pleased with the work we've produced. I think it will lead to a lot of developments.'	
Basic	10. 'It hasn't worked that way in my experience.'	
Basic	11. 'Mike, I'd like you to say whether you agree or not.'	
Responsive	12. 'As I remember it, you agreed to send the paperwork with the order because it helps our system. Now the two have not arrived together. I'd still like this to happen in future.'	
Discrepancy	13. 'Jim, when will you have the order ready?'	
Responsive	14. 'What I meant by that is we may not always have the time.'	
Basic	15. 'I realize that you are wanting to move on to the next stage. However, I'd like you to stick with this till the next person arrives.'	
Empathetic	16. 'I suggest we incorporate that into the last section.'	

Table 5.2 *(continued)*

Suggested answer	*Example*	*Your answer*
Basic	17. 'John, when you say things like that, it sounds like you're taking the department for granted. I don't feel happy about that. So in future, I'd like you to check with one of us before committing us to extra work.'	
Negative feelings	18. 'Unless you are prepared to check with us first before committing us to extra work, we won't be prepared to take it on in future.'	
Consequence	19. 'When you say "the operation", which people are you including in that?'	
Responsive	20. 'Shall we work on the list separately and then check our results at the end?'	
Responsive	21. 'I know you haven't liked working with Pete, but I believe the two of you would be the best ones to sort out the "new design" problems.'	
Empathetic	22. 'On the whole, I go along with that idea as long as we can iron out a few problems with it.'	
Basic	23. 'On the one hand you have agreed to improve the arrangements for our department, but now you are dismissing the problems we raise. I'd like to get clear where we stand.'	
Discrepancy	24. Margaret, why do you think it will cause problems?'	
Responsive	25. 'You're still taking a long time with the first part, which means I have to rush the second part to get it all out on time. I'm feeling irritated by this, so I'd like you to suggest what we can do to speed up the first part.'	
Negative feelings		

6. Handling negative feelings

Managers often say to us they have succeeded in making changes in their *behaviour*—so for much of the time they can behave assertively—but there are still times when they have such strong negative *feelings* that they have difficulty in being assertive. This may have happened to you also. For instance, have you experienced any of the following:
- Feeling angry about a sarcastic remark from someone and responding with an aggressive retort which leads to a prolonged row?
- Feeling worried about your manager's reaction and being unable to ask him for a regrading of your job?
- Feeling very frustrated about the service you are getting from a colleague and blowing your top when you next see him?
- Feeling guilty about imposing on a colleague and not asking her for assistance even though you are rushed off your feet?

The above statements, while not necessarily reflecting your feelings accurately, may have prompted you to think of similar incidents and the accompanying feelings. What is important to note is that because of your feelings you then behaved in certain ways.

Some of the feelings you experience—excitement, enthusiasm, confidence, concern—we would call *productive* feelings. They are useful in leading you to behave effectively: preparing systematically, speaking clearly, stating facts as you see them, replying calmly. Some of the feelings—extreme anger, worry, frustration, guilt, jealousy, depression, inadequacy—are much more negative, and we call them *unproductive* feelings. They make it difficult for you to behave effectively and in ways that you would like. So you mumble your words, 'blow your top', back off issues that are important to you, 'run round in circles' when preparing.

Essentially, this book is about developing assertive *behaviour*. But we recognize that, if we deal exclusively with behaviour, then the process of changing would actually take longer. The behaviour changes would be hindered by the strong feelings you would still be experiencing. So this chapter steps back from the behaviour to work on the feelings that affect behaviour. It looks at the way many people handle feelings, where the feelings come from, the nature of thinking processes, and a strategy for handling unproductive feelings.

The way many people handle feelings

Many people believe that feelings are instinctive, part of the total package they start out with at birth. Because of this they think they are 'stuck' with various feelings. You often hear people saying things like 'She easily feels hurt. She can't help it. She's over-sensitive'; or 'She's always feeling angry about something or other. That's Jean for you'. If you believe that feelings are the result of your genetic make up, like the colour of your eyes, then you have only two options when it comes to handling them.

OPTION 1. STIFLE YOUR FEELINGS

By this, people usually mean don't give any outward expression to your emotions. This is also encouraged by various socialization messages like 'We're British, we don't show our emotions'; or 'It's not ladylike to stamp your feet'; and 'Men don't cry'. This idea of suppressing your feelings probably originated at the same time as the Victorian corset—the effects are pretty similar, too! The trouble with stifling your feelings is that they don't actually go away. You merely experience them internally, while externally you exhibit behaviour that is out of line with your feelings. This gap between the behaviour and the feelings creates enormous stress which tends to show itself in headaches, nervous tension, and the like.

OPTION 2. GIVE VENT TO YOUR FEELINGS

This implies expressing your feelings freely in outward behaviour, regardless of when, where, and with whom. Certainly, if you exercise this option you may not suffer the side effects that go with stifling your feelings; but you may well create other problems for yourself, particularly in the reactions you get from other people. It would be a pretty daunting prospect if everyone openly expressed all of his feelings all the time!

Both of these options leave much to be desired, and many people who go for one rather than the other do so because it seems the lesser of two evils. This is the dilemma if you believe feelings are *instinctive*. In the next section we question this belief. This then opens up the possibility of a *third* option for handling unproductive feelings—without the stress of stifling them inwards; without the undesirable repercussions of giving vent to them.

Where feelings come from

SOME FEELINGS ARE INSTINCTIVE

There is controversy among physiologists and psychologists as to what constitutes feelings and where they come from. There is agreement that most of the physiological sensations we experience—heart pounding, shallow breathing, dry mouth—are instinctive, in that they are with us from birth. They are not usually under our conscious control but are automatically triggered in certain situations. For instance, when we hear a strange, loud, and unexpected noise there are automatic increases in our heart rate, blood

71

pressure, and rate of breathing. All these prepare the body to act for our survival by 'fighting' or 'fleeing'.

SOME FEELINGS ARE LEARNED

Feelings such as anger, hurt, and worry may be accompanied by various of our inborn physiological sensations. It is likely also that these feelings have been developed during a lengthy process of learning from experience. It is difficult to say categorically which feelings are inborn and which are learned, but there is general agreement that we were not born feeling jealous, guilty, or nervous. So how do these feelings arise? Let us answer this question first with two examples, and then with a diagram of what is happening in the examples.

Example 1

Situation	You are on your way to speak to a client who has complained about one of the machines your firm installed recently. He has previously taken up a lot of your time with similar complaints.
Your thinking process	'It's typical of people like him. He's a nuisance. He just likes complaining. He's no right to take up my time like this. I won't let him rabbit on at length.'
Your feelings	Frustration, anger, impatience
Your behaviour	You don't really listen to his complaints to see if they are valid. You interrupt him and give the impression that you need to be away. (*aggression*)

Example 2

Situation	You are about to give a presentation to a group of senior managers. You have only done one presentation before.
Your thinking process	'Presentations are pretty demanding. All these managers will know more than me. They'll try and catch me out. I'll never be able to answer their questions. That will be awful.'
Your feelings	Worry, inadequacy, panic, helplessness
Your behaviour	Stumbling over your words, hesitating: 'I, er, hope you see what I mean . . . only I thought, . . . er, . . . it might . . .' (*nonassertion*)

The diagram in Figure 6.1 represents what is happening in these and similar situations.

Figure 6.1

THE IMPLICATIONS OF THIS MODEL

The total process, of course, is more complex than this, in that there are loopbacks from your feelings to your thinking process, which in turn have a spiralling effect on your feelings. However, what this model implies is that:

– Your feelings do *not* arise 'out of the blue'; they come about as a *result* of an external situation and your thinking process.

– Your feelings are *not* controlled by events or other people; they are controlled by you and your thinking processes.

If this was not so, then you would be at the entire mercy of events and other people. You would be blaming them for how you felt; they would be in control of you—a pretty dreary prospect.

But the examples and the model suggest that it is your *thinking process* about the situation that affects the type and strength of the feelings you have—for instance, whether you feel deep anxiety or only concern. The exciting thing about this proposition is that it opens up the opportunity for you to *gain more control* of your feelings—not to stifle them or to give them a free rein, but to modify or change them in any way you want, and even to express them openly and honestly in an *assertive* way (for example, using 'negative feelings assertion' described in Chapter 5). Just as you can bring your *behaviour* into your conscious control, so you can bring your *feelings* into your control and make them your responsibility.

You may be saying to yourself, if people *do* have this choice over their feelings, how come they choose to have *unproductive* feelings?

WHY PEOPLE HAVE UNPRODUCTIVE FEELINGS

As we have already said, many feelings—both productive and unproductive—occur as a result of thinking processes, which in turn are triggered by external situations. In addition, people frequently experience payoffs for certain of their feelings, that is to say, 'rewards' that follow *after* the feelings. When this happens people repeat those feelings and drop the ones that do not lead to satisfactory payoffs. So over a period of time these rewarded feelings become *learned*—part of the 'feelings repertoire'—even though they may be a hindrance to effective behaviour. The payoffs are sometimes difficult to identify, but we know, for instance, that, strange as it may seem, people can actually *enjoy* feeling helpless, inadequate, rejected, miserable, angry. Maybe the physiological sensations that accompany the feelings are pleasant to experience, or maybe they become familiar. There is also some comfort in the *self-fulfilling* effects of people's behaviour on their beliefs about themselves.

73

Let us give an example of what we mean. If you believe you are a worrier, you will seek to experience worry because this confirms your picture of yourself both in your eyes and other people's.

In addition to wallowing in unproductive feelings, people often find that these feelings lead to behaviours that themselves have short-term payoffs. We have already mentioned this in Chapter 1, so here is just a brief example. Feeling hurt could lead you to say things that frequently succeed in getting people to feel sorry for you, and then to give way to you.

BY WAY OF SUMMARY
So far we have said:
- Some feelings are productive, in that they lead to effective behaviour.
- Some feelings are unproductive, leading to ineffective behaviour.
- Some feelings, like physiological sensations such as heart pounding, are inborn and are not usually under conscious control.
- Some feelings, like jealousy, guilt, and worry, are learned as a result of experiences and the possible payoffs that accompany them.
- These feelings follow after external situations and thinking processes, rather than being caused by situations or other people.
- These feelings can be brought under conscious control.

Of course, feelings that occur out of force of habit become so deeply rooted that you may not realize you can actually make choices about them. The thinking process that leads to these feelings occurs so rapidly that you may not always be aware it exists. In the next section we look more closely at the nature of this thinking process, and in the last section we show how to intervene in the thinking process in order to gain more control over feelings.

Meanwhile you might find it useful to break off at this stage to try out this exercise:
- Think back to a time when, as a result of a particular situation, your feelings were very strong and you behaved less effectively than you would have liked—either aggressively or nonassertively.
- What was the *situation* that triggered it all off; what might you have been *thinking* about the situation; what were the *feelings* you experienced?

The nature of the thinking process

We use the phrase 'thinking process' to refer to all of the things you think about a situation. The thinking process is specific to a particular situation and is triggered, as we have said, in response to that situation. It can be triggered before a situation, during, or after it. Initially we will concentrate on the thinking process that takes place before a situation, because, as you will see in the next section, these are easier to bring under your conscious control to start

74

with. So, your thinking process *before* a situation can consist of any or all of the following thoughts, not necessarily in this order:
– *Memory* of a similar past situation
– *Image* of the situation in question, of yourself and others in the situation
– *Rights* and other people's rights in the situation (for detail on general and job rights, see Chapter 3)
– *Obligations* and how you should appear to others; their obligations to you or to others
– *Anticipation* of your/their behaviour in that situation
– Possible *consequences* for you of these behaviours

Let us give an example of the thinking process in action, together with the resultant feelings and behaviour. The situation we have chosen is a frequent one we experience as trainers and may be familiar to you in your work—giving a presentation to a group of managers. So let us assume you are giving a presentation next week.

Your possible thinking process

'That previous presentation was a disaster. There were lots of awkward questions that I struggled to answer.'

Memory of a similar past experience

↓

'The presentation will be very tough. It's testing my expertise. I'll be on show.'

Image of the situation and yourself within it

↓

'They have no right to try and catch me out. I have the right to get my own back if they do.'

Their rights/your rights in the situation

↓

'I must have all the correct answers. I have to look as though I know my stuff.'

Your obligations/the way you should appear.

↓

'They'll all ask lots of difficult questions; they always do. They'll disagree with my answers.'

Anticipation of their behaviour

↓

'I'll get sucked into lots of arguments that I will lose. That would undermine my professional standing and I can't have that.'

Consequences of their behaviour

↓

'I'll really show them up if they try to catch me out.'

Anticipation of your behaviour

Your likely feelings
These could vary from anger and resentment to determination and even stubbornness.

Your probable behaviour

You would tend to select material that impresses rather than helps understanding.	*Before the presentation*
You would be likely to curtail any discussion abruptly, and respond to 'innocent' questions with put-downs like 'Since when have I said that?'	*During the presentation*

(aggression)

SOUND THINKING PROCESSES

Some of the thoughts you have are *sound*, in that they are a rational, honest, and reasonably accurate reflection of the situation. When this is so they result in feelings—like enthusiasm, excitement, happiness, regret, annoyance, mild frustration, concern, sadness, confidence—that are productive. They goad you into assertive behaviour—into taking appropriate action—that gives you control over yourself and over the situation.

FAULTY THINKING PROCESSES

Some of the thoughts you have are *faulty*, like most of the ones in the above example, in that they are an irrational, not always honest, and often inaccurate reflection of the situation. These faulty thinking processes result in feelings—like extreme anger, resentment, jealousy, rage, deep frustration, worry, pity, helplessness, despair, depression—that are unproductive. They lead you into nonassertive or aggressive behaviour—either into taking no action or inappropriate action—that takes the control away from yourself.

WHAT MAKES SOME THINKING PROCESSES FAULTY?

We ask you to look at Table 6.1 for some answers to this question. There we have taken the *faulty* aspects of the thinking process from the above example and set out the flaws in these, together with some challenges to them.

To sum up, many thinking processes are faulty because
- They deal in extremes and exaggerations such as 'all', 'everyone', 'disaster', 'catastrophe', 'awful', 'terrible'.
- They reach conclusions about the 'inevitability' of things.
- They make generalizations from scant evidence of one event, or one or two people, with labels like: 'typical'; 'they're all the same'.
- They ignore some aspects of the situation.
- They deal in absolutes of right/wrong, black/white, good/bad.
- They place unrealistic expectations on people and on events such as: 'I must'; 'I have to'; 'I ought'; 'They must'; 'They shouldn't'; 'It's not fair'.

76

Table 6.1. Challenges to faulty thinking processes

Faulty thinking process	Flaw	Challenge
That previous presentation was a disaster.	Exaggeration	Is this accurate? Or did only parts of it go badly?
The presentation will be tough.	Generalizing from one event	Is this inevitable just because the previous one was tough?
It's testing my expertise. I'll be on show.	Ignoring important aspects	This may be the most important aspect to you but not necessarily to others.
They have no right to try and catch me out. I have the right to get my own back if they do.	Denying all rights Confusing rights	But don't they have the right to ask questions? Even if people have denied your rights, does this give you the right to stand up for your rights aggressively?
I must have all the correct answers. I have to look as though I know my stuff.	Unrealistic expectations that follow some hidden 'rule book'	Why? What is so terrible about – Being wrong sometimes? – Not having all the answers? – Not knowing something?
They'll all ask lots of difficult questions. They always do.	Assumptions generalizing	Are the 'all' and 'lots' guaranteed, or might it be 'some'? Will the questions necessarily be difficult?
They'll disagree with my answers.	Illogical conclusion	Is this bound to be so?
I'll get sucked into lots of arguments that I will lose.	Exaggeration and assumption	'Lots' or only some arguments? Will you necessarily lose them?
That would undermine my professional standing and I can't have that.	Illogical	Is this probable, or merely possible? Totally or only slightly?
I'll really show them up if they try to catch me out.	Relinquishing control of yourself	Or could you respond assertively if you chose to?

In the next section we show how to deal with faulty thinking processes in order to gain control over unproductive feelings which push you into nonassertion or aggression (as in the example above).

Handling unproductive feelings

People can be successful in modifying and changing their feelings without stifling them or giving vent to them. There are various strategies for this, but the one we have personally found useful, and the one many managers find practical, is to *intervene* in the thinking process. As we have said earlier, the thinking process usually occurs so rapidly that you may not always be aware of it. So one way to slow it down is to intervene with what we will call an *inner dialogue*, that is, talking your thinking process over to yourself.

INTERVENING WITH AN INNER DIALOGUE BEFORE A SITUATION
The diagram in Figure 6.2 shows how the intervention works. We are going to concentrate on using inner dialogue before a situation. This will enable you to control your feelings prior to the situation so that your behaviour both before and during the situation will more likely be assertive. The intervention is easiest to practise at this stage because you get more time to slow down the thinking process. Table 6.2 gives more detail on the steps of the intervention already outlined in Figure 6.2. We invite you to try it out.

Table 6.3 gives examples of working through the intervention strategy in two different situations. These examples are derived from our own and other

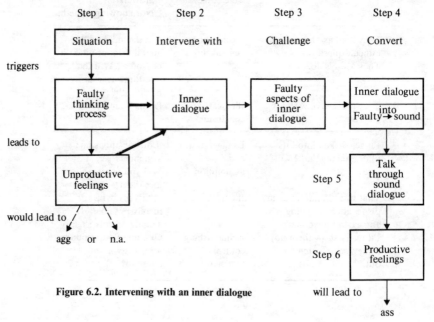

Figure 6.2. Intervening with an inner dialogue

Table 6.2. Intervention strategy before a situation

Steps	Notes
1. Identify a situation	Concentrate on a situation: – That you initiate yourself or know of in advance – That is likely to happen in the next week – That you know will give rise to strong feelings and thus will make it difficult for you to behave assertively (you may know this from similar situations in the past) (A likely situation could be: a meeting, your appraisal, appraising your staff, raising a difficult issue with your manager, a colleague or a customer.)
2. Start the intervention	After identifying a situation you may already be started on your thinking process, or experiencing strong unproductive feelings, so *intervene with your inner dialogue*. In other words, talk through your thinking process to yourself. Do not veto your faulty thinking at this stage—it is a good idea to get your *worst* thinking out into your dialogue. So your dialogue may be a mixture of faulty and sound elements. Make sure it contains at least: your anticipated behaviour; their anticipated behaviour; and the consequences of these for you. These should include the worst that could happen (Table 6.3 gives examples of what we mean).
3. Challenge faulty inner dialogue	Challenge all the faulty elements by looking out for exaggerations, assumptions, and the like (see Tables 6.1 and 6.3 for examples of challenges).
4. Convert faulty dialogue into sound dialogue	Retain any sound elements. Replace all the faulty elements with corresponding sound ones. Be certain that your sound dialogue includes at least: your rights; their rights in the situation; and your anticipated behaviour. The aim is not to give yourself a 'pep' talk with statements of the impossible, but to be realistic and rational (Table 6.3 has examples of sound dialogue).
5. Talk through the sound dialogue	Talk through the sound inner dialogue to yourself until you are comfortable and familiar with it (out loud is even better).
6. Describe your feelings	Try and describe what you now feel about the situation. Your feelings should be of the *productive* variety, e.g., concern, confidence, irritation, excitement, enthusiasm, annoyance, sadness, happiness, etc. If not, then you may still have a lurking faulty inner dialogue that needs challenging more strongly. Or you may need to repeat your sound dialogue to yourself once more. The aim is to *modify* any strong unproductive feelings, *not* to change them dramatically. For instance, it is better to modify deep anxiety into concern rather them try to feel carefree!

Table 6.3. Examples of intervention strategy before a situation

Situation	Possible faulty inner dialogue	Challenge	Sound inner dialogue
1. John, a subordinate, has again made mistakes in the invoices. You have told him before about this. You are about to see him.	There'll be a row this time.	Is this inevitable?	There'll probably be an uncomfortable exchange.
	He has no right to make a mess of these invoices.	Are you denying him his rights?	He has the right to make mistakes. He has the responsibility not to keep repeating them.
	I have the right to really tear him off a strip.	Violating his rights just because he seems to be violating yours?	I have the right to get him to improve and to accept his responsibility.
	He doesn't care. It's typical of his generation. He'll make some excuse just to 'fob me off'.	'Care' and 'typical' based on what evidence? Is an 'excuse' 100% certain to happen?	He may not care, but that need not hinder his work. There may be excuses, but they need not 'fob me off'. There may be reasons behind the excuses.
	That would totally undermine my position.	Are you really that vulnerable?	That might affect me a little.
	I can't have that. I'll show him. I'll get really mad.	Who is in control of you?	*I can* stand it if I choose to. *I can* point out the effects of his mistakes without getting mad.
	↓		↓
	unproductive feelings—rage vindictiveness		productive feelings— annoyance
	↓		↓
	aggressive behaviour —'Why can't you get this right? I've told you before. . .'		assertive behaviour —'. . . these mistakes are causing me problems . . . Why are they occurring?'

Table 6.3 *(continued)*

Situation	Possible faulty inner dialogue	Challenge	Sound inner dialogue
2. You have a report to finish by the end of the week.	This report will be circulated to a lot of people.		
	Some of them are senior to me. They'll know more about it than me.	Is this necessarily so?	Some of them might know more than me.
	This means they are more capable than me.	Does this follow?	Knowing more doesn't make them more capable.
	They'll pick holes in it. They'll pull it to bits.	All of them? Is this ignoring some aspects of the situation?	Some of them may criticize it; some may like it.
	That would be dreadful.	Would it?	It will be disappointing if some don't like it, but not dreadful.
	I've got to get every word right.	Is this realistic?	It would be nice to get it word perfect, but this isn't realistic.
	I mustn't leave anything out.	What if something were left out?	Some of the less important things could be left out.
	I'll never get it sorted out. ↓ unproductive feelings—hopelessness, panic ↓ nonassertive behaviour—oscillating between frantic disorganized activity and long periods of inactivity	Never?	It may take time but *I can* sort it out. ↓ productive feelings—concern confidence ↓ assertive behaviour —writing an *acceptable* first draft and improving it if time

people's experiences of using the intervention strategy. So they may not ring true for you—your own examples will be more real. Your examples may not contain as much detail as ours. This does not matter, because we were merely covering many possibilities for demonstration purposes. What is important is for you to include in your sound dialogue statements about your anticipated behaviour of the '*I can*' variety. These need to be a realistic reflection of your capabilities, so that they push you into planning your behaviour—exactly what you will say and do. You can then rehearse your assertive behaviour to yourself.

As you become accustomed to using the intervention strategy of inner dialogues you will find that you will make less use of Step 3—'challenge'; instead, you automatically convert faulty dialogue into sound. Gradually you get to the point where inner dialogues consist of fewer faulty thoughts anyway. Using an inner dialogue intervention *before* a situation soon has a spin off effect on you *during* a situation.

INTERVENING DURING A SITUATION

To be realistic, you would be unlikely to intervene in the thinking process *during* a situation until you were practised at doing it *before* a situation. Even then, the thinking process happens so quickly during most interactions that you would not have time to work through all the steps of the intervention in Table 6.2. Nevertheless, it is possible to intervene, especially during situations where you went through the full intervention strategy beforehand. Table 6.4 sets out this shorter intervention. There are examples in Table 6.5 of sound inner dialogues for using during an interaction.

Table 6.4. Intervention strategy during a situation

Steps	Notes
1. Take a deep breath	While the other person is talking or just before you respond.
2. Recall your sound dialogue	Talk through at least the part of it that deals with his behaviour and the 'I can' statements. Make them apply to the present instead of the future. (Table 6.5 gives examples of these.)
3. Slow down your response	Do this by starting your response with slow, firm words or phrases such as 'Well', 'I see', 'Let me see', 'Fine', 'Yes'. This buys you time to collect at least your first sentence together.

Table 6.5. Examples of sound inner dialogues during a situation

Situation	Sound inner dialogue
1. Steve, a colleague, is reluctant to agree to firm deadlines. He keeps stating difficulties.	I'm feeling frustrated but I can control it. I can tell Steve why. Then I'll begin to get somewhere. I can repeat my need for firm deadlines. I needn't get impatient.
2. Margaret, a member of staff, is very edgy when you refuse a request for time off.	She's getting upset. She may get angry. That needn't put me off balance. I have the right to refuse. I needn't be rude to her. I can continue to be assertive.

INTERVENING AFTER A SITUATION

If someone bursts into your office giving you no chance to hold an inner dialogue with yourself before the situation and little time during, then it's a good idea to work through one afterwards. Already you might be accustomed to thinking things over as you drive home in the car ('if only I'd said that'). If you find yourself replaying things over and over again and feeling more sick with each replay, then you have a faulty inner dialogue! In Table 6.6 we include some faulty and corresponding sound inner dialogues.

Table 6.6. Inner dialogues after a situation

Situation	Faulty inner dialogue	Sound inner dialogue
1. You put forward your idea to senior managers for a change in reporting levels. They rejected your idea.	It's awful that I can't get senior managers to see why they need to change. It's typical of the narrow view they take. I might as well give up.	If I can't get them to change it is frustrating, but not awful. It may be narrow in my eyes but that doesn't mean it *is* narrow. I can begin to make plans to minimize the effect on me.
2. You started to behave assertively to your colleague but lost it when the going got rough.	I might have known it wouldn't work with Tom. He deserved that—accusing me of lying. He really makes my blood boil.	It will be difficult with Tom but not impossible. Next time I can keep going longer. He may aggravate me, but I needn't rise to the bait. I can keep my cool—I'll take a deep breath next time.

Inner dialogues after a situation enable you to learn from it. So it is important not to gloss over successes as if they were trivial. It is a myth that people learn only from failures. Successes enable you to know what might be worth repeating another time. Similarly, it is useful to analyse failures but not to berate yourself because of them. There are likely to be elements of success and failure in most situations, so why not work to increase the success and reduce the failure?

Summary

In this chapter we have stepped back from observable behaviour and have considered
– How feelings affect behaviour
– How thinking processes lead to feelings
– How to intervene in thinking processes with inner dialogues
– Challenges to faulty inner dialogues
– How to convert a faulty dialogue into a sound one
This enables you to modify unproductive feelings into productive ones and then to behave assertively.

In later chapters we continue to refer to inner dialogues.

7. Giving and receiving criticism about performance

Talking about unsatisfactory aspects of performance is one of the most difficult tasks that people at work have to face—whether they are giving or receiving criticism. It is made difficult because many people almost equate performance of the job with competence as a person. This means that if they see a person, say, as being inadequate at writing reports, then they would also tend to see him as being inadequate as a *person*—clearly an illfounded conclusion. Yet it is often the basis (either for the giver or for the receiver) of much of the criticism of performance that occurs at work. Think how often criticism about job performance turns into an attack upon the person himself; think how often the person concerned perceives himself under attack.

You yourself may have had unwelcome experiences either making or taking criticism. This chapter aims to help you avoid such experiences by introducing some guidelines in giving criticism *assertively*, either to a subordinate or even to a colleague. This is followed by some hints on how to behave assertively when *receiving* criticism.

Giving criticism

When faced with someone's unsatisfactory performance, have you found yourself
– Avoiding raising the particular criticism, or raising it very tentatively?
  (nonassertion)
– Working yourself into an angry state so that you raise the issue in an abrupt, heavy-handed way?
  (aggression)
In these cases, either the required change in the person's performance does not come about, or if it does it is accompanied by some undesirable changes. Maybe the person ends up saying 'OK, if that's what you want me to do in future, I'll do it.' At the same time he is probably *saying to himself*, 'But don't expect me to help out the next time you've got a rush on.' Neither of these is a satisfactory outcome, and likely as not the relationship between you gets worse.

Let us begin by stating that criticizing performance is not an end in itself; it is done to achieve a particular goal. The goal is *a change in the way a person carries out a particular aspect of his job*. It is easy to lose sight of this end and to become addicted to the means. Many people see criticizing itself as the all-important thing; as long as they do this they think they are 'managing'. Criticizing is seen as 'just a matter of a two-minute ticking off, then all will be well'. Sadly, all will most certainly *not* be well. This approach gives criticism a negative feel to it (one of the reasons we hesitated about even using the word in the first place). Let us stress that we see criticism as a *constructive* event—with emphasis on future changes for improvement rather than on the error of past ways; with follow-up afterwards, if necessary, to check progress.

So, armed with this positive rather than destructive image of giving criticism, we will now consider the rights of the people involved.

RIGHTS INVOLVED IN CRITICISM
If you want to use criticism as a legitimate means of helping a person improve his performance, then you are more likely to be effective if you make your criticism assertively. In order to do this you need to accept that you have the *right* to want people to improve their performance. Following on from this, you need to accept the right to criticize that performance. The *responsibility* that goes with this right is to criticize in a way that does not attack the person, put him down, or make him look small. Even though he has made mistakes, repeated mistakes, or failed to improve, he has *not* forfeited his right to be treated assertively. In other words, his mistakes do not give you the right to behave aggressively.

To behave assertively also requires you to have sound inner dialogues about the particular situation and the person you intend to criticize.

SOME COMMON INNER DIALOGUES
In Table 7.1 are some examples of common faulty dialogues concerning giving criticism, and some equivalent sound ones. Faulty dialogues 1–4 will result in your behaving aggressively; 5 and 6 will lead to nonassertion. The last one will result in nonassertion in the short run, but aggression when you do eventually raise the issue with Andy. The first faulty dialogue is an example of violating the rights of someone who has made a mistake.

Faulty dialogue 5 is an example of how the anticipation of the other person's nonassertion influences your behaviour. Faulty dialogue 6 indicates a similar thing with anticipation of aggression. More about this in Chapter 8.

GUIDELINES FOR GIVING CRITICISM
The guidelines we give in Figure 7.1 are intended for use when making those 'everyday' criticisms of performance, for example when someone produces typing that is not to the agreed standard. They can also be used in conjunction with the hints (earlier in the book) for giving praise, because there are usually good as well as bad aspects to a particular piece of work. It would be important to bring out both these aspects when you are dealing with some of the larger parts of a person's job—for instance, a project or a lengthy report.

86

Table 7.1. Inner dialogues about giving criticism

Faulty inner dialogues	*Sound inner dialogues*
1. 'I have the right to really tear John off a strip when I talk to him about the mess he made of his budget forecasts.'	'Just because John has made mistakes, he has not forfeited his right to be treated assertively. I can point out how his budget forecasts affected me.'
2. 'I've spoken to Reg twice before about this. He's just being awkward.'	'I've spoken to Reg twice before about this. I won't assume he is being awkward. He may have forgotten. I can remind him firmly without getting mad.'
3. 'If I give Mike half a chance, he'll start blaming me or others for his poor presentation yesterday. I'll make it clear from the beginning that I'm not going to stand for that.'	'Mike may start blaming me or others. If he does I can listen. Some of his points may be valid. I can get him to see why I think the presentation was poor.'
4. 'It was disastrous that Ann made that mistake.'	'Ann's mistake created real problems but was not disastrous. I can point them out. I can keep my cool. I can get her to change.'
5. 'If I raise this issue with Mary, she's sure to get upset; that would be embarrassing. I would hate that.'	'Mary doesn't *always* get upset when I raise issues of this kind with her. If she does it may be embarrassing, but I can live with that.'
6. 'If I mention his mistakes to him, he's sure to fly off the handle. That would be terrible.'	'Even if he does fly off the handle, I believe I can cope with it.'
7. 'I won't make an issue of it this time, it'll look petty. But if Andy does it again, that will be it.'	'I'll raise it with Andy now, while it's still only a small irritation. He may think it's petty but it will stop a bigger blow up later on.'

The approach we suggest will in most cases be used with the staff working for you, but it can also be used when you are unhappy about an aspect of a colleague's performance—for example, when he is sending his monthly return to you late.

Figure 7.1 summarizes the steps we suggest for giving criticism assertively and includes some examples. Following these steps increases the chances that you will reach agreement on any desired changes.

Notes on the guidelines

Steps 1 and 2. Frequently you will be taking the initiative in raising an issue

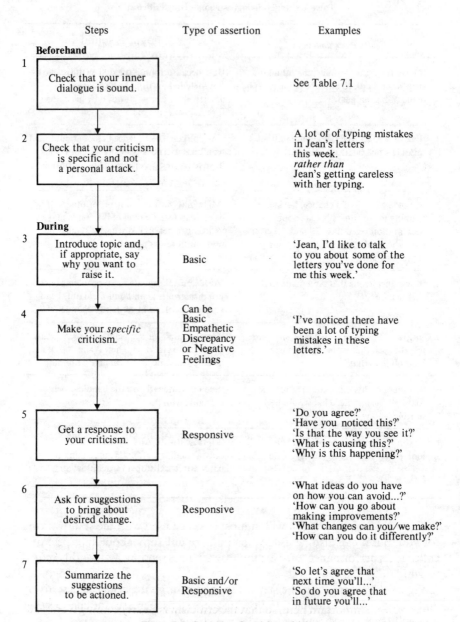

Steps	Type of assertion	Examples
Beforehand		
1 Check that your inner dialogue is sound.		See Table 7.1
2 Check that your criticism is specific and not a personal attack.		A lot of of typing mistakes in Jean's letters this week. *rather than* Jean's getting careless with her typing.
During		
3 Introduce topic and, if appropriate, say why you want to raise it.	Basic	'Jean, I'd like to talk to you about some of the letters you've done for me this week.'
4 Make your *specific* criticism.	Can be Basic Empathetic Discrepancy or Negative Feelings	'I've noticed there have been a lot of typing mistakes in these letters.'
5 Get a response to your criticism.	Responsive	'Do you agree?' 'Have you noticed this?' 'Is that the way you see it?' 'What is causing this?' 'Why is this happening?'
6 Ask for suggestions to bring about desired change.	Responsive	'What ideas do you have on how you can avoid...?' 'How can you go about making improvements?' 'What changes can you/we make?' 'How can you do it differently?'
7 Summarize the suggestions to be actioned.	Basic and/or Responsive	'So let's agree that next time you'll...' 'So do you agree that in future you'll...'

Figure 7.1. Guidelines for giving criticism

with someone. You therefore have time to do a little preparation, even if it is only a matter of two or three minutes before you go and see that person. During this period, you can check that your inner dialogue is sound and your criticism specific. As we have dealt with inner dialogues above, we will say a few more words about making your criticism specific. We suggest you describe as clearly as possible that aspect of a person's *observable behaviour* that you would like to see changed. For example:

– Coming in late in the mornings
– Not following the agreed format when writing a report
– Criticizing members of staff in the presence of others

Expressing criticisms in this factual form helps to ensure that your criticism is not seen as a personal attack. Generalized statements ('You made a mess of that') are too vague for the person to visualize what he has to change. Personalized statements ('You're attitude is all wrong' or 'You're too autocratic') are about traits such as personality or attitudes that not only cannot be observed but are likely to be seen as a personal attack.

Step 3. This is concerned with setting the scene by announcing the topic for discussion *before* getting immersed in the detail of the particular criticism you want to make. This eases the way into the criticism so that it is not seen as a 'bolt from the blue'. (Remember, the other person may have his mind on something else at the time.) It also helps you get to the point of the interaction, rather than beating about the bush. The latter approach smacks of nonassertion and often makes the other person suspicious.

It can also be useful at this step to say why you want to discuss this particular issue. You can do this by:

– Mentioning how the issue has arisen; for instance, 'I've had several managers ringing up to complain about the tone of the circular you sent out last week'
– Pointing out that the shortfall in performance affects you: for example, '. . . because I've had some problems as a result of the circular. . .'
– Pointing out that this shortfall affects the person himself: for instance, '. . . because I think it will affect the co-operation the other departments will give you'

The idea is not to give masses of detail or long complicated explanation at this point.

Step 4. Here you want assertively to make your specific criticism. 'I' statements are important here, so that the criticism is clearly coming from you and not from some anonymous source. So the following phrases are useful:

– 'I noticed in your return last week that . . .'
– 'I'm not happy about the way . . .'
– 'As I see it, you are leaving out . . .'

– 'I think your report isn't . . .'

Such phrases are in contrast to the 'It has been noticed . . .' variety. They also contrast with the blaming phrases, which emphasize the *you* ('You really should have adopted a more conciliatory tone in the circular you sent out last week').

It helps if you keep your criticism short and clear to start with. After that you may want to discuss the effect that the shortfall in performance is having. If you mentioned this briefly in Step 3, then you could explore it in more detail here; for instance, 'I think some of the words you have used will alienate some of the managers and make them less willing to cooperate.'

Apart from the above examples, the type of assertion you use at this stage will depend on the circumstances, and whether you have raised this particular issue before with that person. If it is the first time, you can use a basic assertion. If you know that he is under a lot of pressure at the moment and want him to know that you recognize this, then an empathetic assertion would be appropriate. Discrepancy and negative feelings are higher-level assertions and are best used when you have raised this particular issue before but the desired change in performance has not been made.

It is usually less effective if you make a lot of criticisms at the same time. There is a strict limit to how many changes anyone can work on at any one time. One is enough, two is plenty, and three is the absolute maximum.

The crucial nonverbal behaviour when giving criticism is eye contact. Too little, and the other person will sense you are having difficulty raising the issue and therefore find it easier to ignore or disagree with what you say. Too much (in the form of glaring) will be seen as aggressive.

Step 5. This is concerned with getting *agreement* to your criticism. This is vital before you can go on and agree (in Step 6) what changes to make. Responsive assertion will be the predominant behaviour here—you are asking questions to find out if the other person really agrees with your criticism. If not, he may have valid reasons for seeing it differently. If the person agrees, you will probably want to find out why the shortfall in performance has occurred. So Step 5 gives you opportunity to uncover information that may be new to you. This may mean you need to modify your criticism or even withdraw it. It is aggressive to carry on pursuing your original criticism in the face of such new information.

At this stage you may also discover that the other person is not clear on the standards of performance you expect from him in this part of his job. If this happens, it is assertive to acknowledge your own shortfall here. You would then want to make clear what you expect and to get agreement that such standards are realistic. Pursuing your criticism in such situations again would be aggressive; we do not believe you have the *right* to criticize a person's performance if you have not made your expectations clear to him beforehand.

Step 6. This is where you encourage the other person to come up with suggestions to bring about that change. Again, responsive assertion is the major behaviour ('What ideas do you have. . .?'). You may need to make some suggestions yourself if the other person is having difficulty in seeing how the change could be made. If you do this with someone who tends to behave nonassertively, it is useful to make the suggestion in a responsive form ('How about trying to . . .?' or 'Would it work if you . . .?'). This increases the chances of bringing out into the open any difficulties that the other person may have in implementing these suggestions. By the way, the suggestions that arise may well be about *you* making changes—for instance, in the way you schedule the work.

Step 7. Here you summarize what has been agreed. All too often, people go away clear on what they are *not* going to do, but not so clear on what they *are* going to do. So from the suggestions considered, decide which ones are to be actioned. This last step is crucial if the other person is to leave the interaction clear on the changes that he or you will be making. If you close with a statement about how and when you will monitor and review the success of the changes, then the other person is more likely to take the issue seriously.

In conclusion, the above guidelines are meant to be used flexibly. So, for instance, if one of your staff is not completing part of a monthly return correctly, you may not need to go through Steps 6 and 7; you just make your criticism, ask him to do X rather than Y, and check that he understands and agrees.

Following these guidelines makes it less likely that the other person will become aggressive or nonassertive. Nonassertion is undesirable because the other person will be holding back from stating his views and airing his doubts. This may result in his *apparently* agreeing to do something differently, but then quietly going back to his old ways once your discussion is over. If you suspect the other person *will* become aggressive or nonassertive, Chapters 9 and 10 deal with how to maintain your assertion.

We have talked so far in this chapter about how to *give* criticism assertively. It also requires skill to *receive* criticism assertively, so the next section looks at this area.

Receiving criticism assertively

No doubt you have been on the receiving end of criticism that you felt was not justified, or, if it was justified, was given aggressively. Either way, you may have responded aggressively or nonassertively. It would be wonderful if everyone made their criticism to you assertively, but this is probably unrealistic! So this section is aimed at helping you respond assertively to criticism, whether it is given assertively, aggressively, or nonassertively.

RIGHTS IN RECEIVING CRITICISM

The first issue to consider is that of rights. If you do not accept that the other person has the right to criticize your performance, then, however he goes about it, you will see his behaviour as aggressive. If you accept he has the right, you will want him also to accept *your* rights in this situation—not to be put down, or made to look small or be subjected to personal attacks, and for the criticism to be made in private rather than in front of colleagues.

INNER DIALOGUES

The inner dialogues you have also affect the way you respond to the criticism. Examples of faulty ones are: 'Oh dear, that's another clanger, I'm really bodging this up' or 'He's at it again, always nit-picking, always got to find something wrong'. The former leads you into behaving nonassertively, where you may become over-apologetic or start putting yourself down. The latter pushes you into aggression, because you mentally dismiss what may be valid criticisms before they are even made. So, turn any faulty dialogues you may have into sound ones. For instance: 'I may have made a mistake but not necessarily a complete bodge', or 'The criticism may be a personal attack. I can dig behind that. I can learn from criticism.'

HINTS FOR RECEIVING CRITICISM

Unclear criticism

If you are not clear exactly what the criticism is, you can ask the other person for clarification and for him if possible to give you an example. It is important to do this assertively and not in a challenging way that will be heard as 'go on, I bet you can't think of an example to back up your charge'. Both basic assertions (especially the 'I' statements part) and responsive assertions are useful here. For example: 'I'd like you to give me some examples of what you mean, Pete', or 'What sort of thing were you thinking of?' or 'Can you give me some specific instances/examples, Steve?'

Personal attack

If the criticism is made in the form of a personal attack, try and separate in your mind the content (which may be valid) from the way it is given. If such personal attacks have happened before and you want to bring your unease about this to the other person's attention, you can say things like 'I accept that your criticism may be valid, John. However, I'd prefer it if you made it less of a personal attack.'

You disagree with the criticism
If you do not accept the criticism, then it is assertive to say so. 'I' statements are important in keeping the interaction on an assertive/assertive level. ('As *I* see it, the . . .')

No agreement on future changes
As it is in your interest that suggestions are agreed for the future, you can take the initiative in this area, if the other person appears content to end the interaction before this has been done.

Nonverbal behaviour
Throughout the interaction it is important to maintain steady eye contact. You also need to keep your voice up rather than letting it sink as if you are being deflated. Something else to avoid is letting your voice get high-pitched ('You never told me *that!*'). These suggest that you are on the defensive. Your assertion encourages assertion in the other person.

By following these hints and guidelines you can become more assertive in giving and receiving criticism. Then, like praise, it will become much more an everyday event, carried out in a matter of fact way and causing very few ripples.

8. How others influence you

So far in the book we have concentrated on developing skills for behaving assertively in various situations. However, we recognize that this assertiveness could well break down when 'the going gets rough'—when other people behave aggressively or nonassertively towards you. So the emphasis in these next three chapters is on how you can remain assertive in the light of their aggression and nonassertion. We start the process in this chapter by looking at how other people's behaviour (in the form of ass, agg, or n.a.) influences you. We do this by following through a detailed example. In the following two chapters we show how to handle other people's aggression and nonassertion respectively.

What we mean by influence

It is inevitable when you are interacting with others, whether at work or in your social life, that you will try to influence them. In turn they will try to influence you. We define 'influencing' quite simply as having an effect upon someone. This could mean having an effect on what someone thinks, feels, says, or does. Some of the influence exercised between people is *not legitimate* as far as assertiveness is concerned, because it violates assertive rights. Thus it is not assertive to influence people in any matters—their likes, dislikes, opinions, interests, decisions, actions—that do *not affect* you, but it is a legitimate part of assertiveness to give yourself the right to influence people in matters that do affect you. Alongside this, there is the responsibility of influencing people 'openly': by being assertive rather than aggressive or nonassertive. In addition, it is legitimate to give people the right to influence you in matters that affect them. Unfortunately, they will not always do this assertively but will sometimes use aggression or nonassertion. Later we look at the effects of these three forms of influence on you.

THE TWO ELEMENTS OF INFLUENCE
Other people have two strings to their bow when it comes to influencing you.
– They have the facts, opinions, and suggestions they put forward (we will call these the *content*).
– They have the *way* they put these facts, opinions, and suggestions forward (we call this the *behaviour*).
The following example illustrates what we mean by these two elements.
  In a meeting you put forward a suggestion on changes to the maintenance schedule and a colleague, Mike, says, in a matter of fact tone: 'If you do that,

breakdowns will increase and it will be more difficult for us to hit the production targets.'

Here Mike is using the *content*—the facts and opinions—as his primary means of influencing you. Now suppose that, instead of the above reply, Mike had raised his voice and said: 'Oh come on, that's nonsense and you know it. If you do that breakdowns will go through the roof and we'll never hit target.'

Here Mike would be using the *behaviour* (aggression) as his primary means of influencing you. We are concerned in this chapter with the way others use the *behaviours* of aggression, nonassertion and assertion to influence you. We consider the effect of these behaviours on you by following through an example of decision making. We have chosen decision making because this is an area in which others are particularly keen to influence you.

How aggression from others influences you

Let us assume that, after weighing up all the facts and sounding out the people affected, you have decided to make changes to the organization structure of two of the departments that come under your control. You recognize that, whatever decisions you come to, you will not please everyone. You are now at the point of presenting the proposed changes to the staff of these departments.

After your initial presentation of these changes, Norman (a member of staff who has long been a thorn in your flesh) challenges your statement about increased efficiency coming from the re-organization. He does this pretty aggressively, and goes on to point out a couple of problems in making the proposed changes work. He ends up by making a sarcastic reference to some of the other changes you have made.

Unless you are practised at assertively handling aggression, Norman's aggressive behaviour is likely to influence you along one of two routes— nonassertion or aggression. Roughly what happens is this. The emotional overtone of Norman's aggression hooks your own emotions. This happens either because you have not intervened in your *thinking process*, or because you have intervened with a *faulty inner dialogue*. Your own feelings that come to the fore are negative ones, which lead you either into nonassertion or into aggression. Figure 8.1 illustrates this.

We will examine each of the two routes in turn.

WHEN YOU RESPOND NONASSERTIVELY
If you feel embarrassed by Norman's attack in front of a group of your staff, then you may behave nonassertively perhaps by going too far to placate him. To do this you might change your proposals on the reorganization, so that they now meet his needs, but not necessarily yours. When this happens, you are making the changes not because of the content of what he says—the problems he raises—but because of the behaviour he uses. When this occurs,

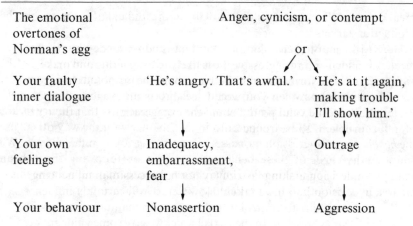

Figure 8.1. How the other person's aggression affects you

Norman's attempt to influence you to change your decision has been successful. The important thing to note is that the emotional overtones of the other person's behaviour have lead you into *countering* that behaviour with emotional behaviour of your own (in this case, nonassertion). When this happens, the *content of the behaviour often gets overlooked.* So in the above example the problems Norman raised may or may not be valid but, because your energy goes into countering his behaviour, you may not examine the content at all.

So, in addition to influencing you to change the decision, the other person has also *influenced you to change your behaviour*—from assertion to nonassertion. He is beginning to control your behaviour as well as the decisions you take.

WHEN YOU RESPOND AGGRESSIVELY
If you feel yourself 'bristling' during Norman's attack, then you will most probably respond aggressively. One way to do this is to make a personal attack upon Norman. Another is to make it clear to Norman that you have no intention of changing your proposals, whatever he or anyone else says. Either of these responses will tend to deter any other member of your staff from identifying any potential problems with your proposed changes.

In responding in this way you have again put your energy into countering Norman's behaviour. You are responding to his aggressive behaviour with aggression. But this time his attempt to *influence you to change your decision is unsuccessful*. However, because his aggressive behaviour has hooked your aggression, he *has been successful in influencing you to change your behaviour*. With you putting your energy into countering his behaviour, you are in danger of giving little or no attention to the validity of the content of his contribution.

Thus, you may be lumbering yourself with an organizational structure that has real problems associated with it.

This problem of overlooking the content is compounded by the fact that, when a person is being aggressive, he is likely to exaggerate and make extreme statements. So if Norman said something about the proposed changes causing *enormous* problems, then you would see this as an exaggeration. You can easily overlook the valid point behind the exaggeration—that there may well be *some* problems to be ironed out.

IN SUMMARY

Other people's aggression may or may not be successful in influencing you to change a decision you have taken. However, it will certainly influence your behaviour, and start to control it, unless you can maintain your assertion in the face of this aggression. In the next chapter we give some guidelines on how to do this.

How nonassertion from others influences you

You may well have experienced people using aggression to influence you. You may not be so aware that others use nonassertion to the same end. Nonassertion is less dramatic, and less apparent, than aggression. Nevertheless (or maybe because of this!) it can be just as effective in influencing you. Let us return to our example from the previous section, where you have made a decision about organizational changes. Instead of Norman being aggressive, you have a colleague of his, Don, behaving nonassertively when you ask him for his view of the proposed changes. He says something like: 'Well, we do have a lot on at the moment . . . and, er, these changes are bound to take up some of our time. But I suppose we'll try and manage somehow.'

Again, *unless you are practised at responding assertively to nonassertion*, then Don's nonassertion will influence you to respond in one of two ways: nonassertively or aggressively. What happens here is that the overtones of Don's behaviour contain a sort of 'emotional blackmail'. We use the word blackmail in the sense that the emotion can be fairly insidious; it doesn't 'hit you as hard' as aggressive emotion. But nevertheless, it will be just as effective in hooking your own feelings, which in turn lead you to behave nonassertively or aggressively. We illustrate how this happens in Figure 8.2. We will explore each of these two alternatives in more detail.

WHEN YOU RESPOND NONASSERTIVELY

If you start feeling guilty for making additional demands upon Don, this is because his nonassertion has lead you to have a faulty inner dialogue. What you say to yourself and what you feel will lead you to behave nonassertively. For instance, you might put off the date for implementing the changes in

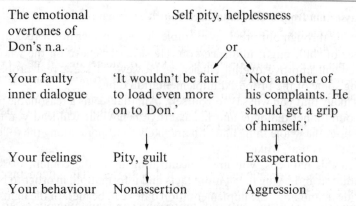

The emotional overtones of Don's n.a.	Self pity, helplessness or	
Your faulty inner dialogue	'It wouldn't be fair to load even more on to Don.'	'Not another of his complaints. He should get a grip of himself.'
Your feelings	Pity, guilt	Exasperation
Your behaviour	Nonassertion	Aggression

Figure 8.2. How the other person's nonassertion affects you

Don's section with the result that your needs are no longer met. So *Don's behaviour*, his nonassertion—rather than the content of his statement—*has influenced you to change the decision.*

In addition, Don's *nonassertion has influenced you to change your behaviour*, from assertion to nonassertion. You are moving away from controlling your own behaviour.

As with responding to aggression, when you put energy into countering the emotions associated with the other person's nonassertion you tend to give less attention to the content of the statement. So in the example you may not check the validity of Don's problems or whether they can be overcome without major changes to your decision.

WHEN YOU RESPOND AGGRESSIVELY

This can come about because your faulty inner dialogue leads you to feel exasperated with Don's nonassertion. For instance, you may see his statement about the workload as just one more in a long line of nonassertive complaints from him. Then your exasperation will spill over into aggressive retorts like: 'Don, how come that, whenever I ask you about workload, you tell me you've never been so busy. Isn't it about time you got on top of things?'

When this occurs you are ceasing to listen to the content of Don's contribution to see if it is valid, and you are again responding to his behaviour. If there is a real problem with implementing the required changes while coping with the heavy workload, then you have failed to pick it up.

So Don's attempt to influence you with nonassertion to change the decision has failed. But he has influenced you to change your behaviour, from assertion to aggression—thus removing some of your control over yourself.

In Chapter 10 we give some hints for responding assertively to nonassertion. But now we will look at assertion influencing you.

How assertion from others influences you

Following through our previous example, let us consider how Mike, another member of staff, might influence you. He says: 'I believe on the whole the changes will improve overall efficiency. However, I see a real problem in meeting some of the proposed implementation dates.'

It is likely that you will say to yourself, 'Ah, that seems a reasonable point.' This sound inner dialogue and his assertive behaviour will lead you to feel calm about the whole thing and you are likely to respond along the following lines: 'Why is that, Mike?'

When this happens, you are concentrating upon the content of Mike's contribution and trying to get more facts and information, in order to be able to decide if, and how, the implementation dates can be met. In the light of the information that comes out you will be able to take a more objective rather than emotional decision about whether to modify any of the implementation dates.

This comes about because there are no negative feelings accompanying Mike's behaviour, so it makes it easier for you to conduct the discussion on an assertive–assertive level. We summarize this in Figure 8.3.

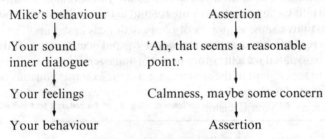

Figure 8.3. How assertion affects you

Mike may or may not be successful in influencing you to change the decision. This will not matter. What matters is that, if the decision is changed or if it remains unaltered, *this will be in the light of the content of what the other person says.*

Before moving on to handle aggression and nonassertion in Chapters 9 and 10, we would like to examine a particularly powerful way in which people can influence you.

How people influence you through their past behaviour

In addition to people influencing you through their present behaviour of aggression, nonassertion and assertion, *people can also influence you through their past behaviour.* We will again refer to decision making in order to demonstrate this. In the previous examples all the attempts to influence you occurred *after* you made your decision. This time we will look at how people can influence you *before* you make a decision.

Of course, you may be well aware of people trying to influence you before you make a decision—when they come to you 'lobbying' you; when you go to them collecting information, say, about alternatives. You probably realize that people usually have more to gain by influencing you before you make a decision. They can influence you to decide on one particular alternative as opposed to another; whereas, after you have made a decision, their influence is usually restricted to getting modifications to the alternative you have chosen.

What you may not be so conscious of is that people can influence you before you even talk to anyone—*while you are still thinking about a decision.* Let us give an example of this.

Suppose in the past you have been on the end of aggression from a colleague, Brian, when you have taken a decision that was not to his liking. Then you may have a faulty dialogue at work along the lines of 'I would really like to make that change, but if I do Brian will get really annoyed. I don't want to upset him again. It's a pity, but I think I had better hold fire on that.'

The interesting point here is that Brian does not need to *behave* aggressively towards you this time round. He is influencing you successfully through the faulty inner dialogue you are carrying around as the result of past experiences.

Table 8.1 gives some examples of faulty dialogues based upon experiences of people's past reaction. Faulty dialogues 1 and 3 will lead you to behave nonassertively; 2 and 4 will lead you to behave aggressively.

Table 8.1. Faulty dialogues about decision making, based on people's past behaviour

Faulty inner dialogues

1. 'They'll never stand for it. If I go ahead and do that I'll be really unpopular. That would be terrible.'
2. 'Who do they think they are, always trying to veto my decisions? I'm the manager. They'll do what I decide.'
3. 'It wouldn't be fair to Ian if I decide to make changes now. He won't say so but I know he'll be worried.'
4. 'You can't be liked and get things done in this job. Making tough decisions is what I'm paid for.'

Summary

When people influence you, or have influenced you in the past with assertion it makes it easier for you to respond assertively to them. At these times you can concentrate on the content of their behaviour. When people influence you, or have influenced you in the past with aggression or nonassertion, it makes it

100

more difficult for you to respond assertively. This is because the negative feelings accompanying their behaviours get in the way of the content.

In Chapters 9 and 10 we show how to handle aggression and nonassertion assertively. This means that you will be more likely to retain control of your behaviour. In addition, you will be influenced only by the validity of the content of what the other person says.

9. Handling aggression from others

You are not alone if you find it difficult to cope with aggression from others. Many managers feel that highly aggressive exchanges leave them emotionally drained and saying to themselves: 'There must be a better way of handling it.' If you can remember saying things like this to yourself, it is probable that when faced with aggression your response was to be aggressive or nonassertive. We said in Chapter 8 that it is very easy for your response to aggression to go in one of these two ways and we explained how these two responses result from other people *succeeding* in influencing your *behaviour* with their aggression.

In this chapter we show how to respond assertively to aggression and thus retain control of your own behaviour. We will begin by a brief recap of some of the different levels of aggression, some of which we have mentioned in earlier chapters.

Different levels of aggression
We find it useful to draw a distinction between higher levels of aggression and lower levels of aggression.

HIGHER-LEVEL AGGRESSION
This usually takes the form of *personal attacks*, as shown in these examples:

– 'That's not true and you jolly well know it!'
– 'You've been making life difficult for me whenever you've had the slightest chance. I'm really sick of it!'
– 'That's just typical of you! I might have known you'd come up with another tin pot scheme. Just like the last time. . .'

Personal attacks indicate that people are personalizing the differences that exist between themselves and others. So, instead of attacking the issue, they attack the person. People who are high on aggression are fond of using these behaviours because they fit in with their beliefs about other people being out to get them and win at their expense. Exchanges involving personal attacks can often become quite lengthy.

LOWER-LEVEL AGGRESSION

This can take various forms, some of which are:

		Comments
Sarcasm	'What's this masterpiece, then?'	These can become very 'clever' and cutting
Blaming	'It's all Engineering's fault.'	Often contain exaggerations
Dismissing the person/his statement	Dismissive hand gesture; sometimes a sneer 'No. That won't work.'	May show contempt
Patronizing	'It won't be all that bad once you get going. You'll see.'	Treating the other person like a child, condescending. Often shows up in praise

This lower level can also consist of: not listening to you, or hogging the conversation. The lower-level aggressions will not usually extend into a lengthy exchange unless they accompany personal attacks.

Later in the chapter we have guidelines for handling the higher level of aggression, and an exercise for dealing with the lower levels. In the next section we start to cross the barriers that exist between previous ways of handling aggression and future assertive ways.

Overcoming barriers to responding assertively

We believe that the most useful way to improve your handling of other people's aggression is to start with someone who has previously been aggressive to you and whom you think is likely to be aggressive in the future. There are probably a number of *barriers* preventing you from changing the way you handle aggression from this person—most notably your inner dialogue and your feelings. We suggest you begin by tackling these barriers right now.

To start with, recall one or two occasions when you did not handle an aggressive attack from this person as well as you would have liked. (You may have behaved nonassertively, perhaps becoming apologetic or going on the defensive. Or you may have used aggression, saying things you later regretted.) Make a note of your inner dialogues—the things you are saying to yourself—as you think back to the previous incidents and think forward to future aggressive attacks from this person. Also take note of the feelings you experience.

The vital thing in removing any barriers of this sort is to change any faulty dialogues into sound ones and to check that your feelings are productive rather than negative. Here are some examples of the sort of thing you might come up with.

103

IF YOU PREVIOUSLY USED AGGRESSION

Inner dialogue	Type	You feel	Leading to
'I really made a fool of myself then. Whatever must the others think of me now? I'd better keep quiet next time.'	Faulty	Embarrassment, guilt, or shame	Future nonassertion
'I did get a bit steamed up there but he asked for it. I'll get mad again if he behaves like that.'	Faulty	Justified	Future aggression
'I'm disappointed I let myself get into that slanging match. Next time he behaves like that I'll count to 10 before responding.'	Sound	Disappointment mixed with confidence	Future assertion

IF YOU PREVIOUSLY USED NONASSERTION

Inner dialogue	Type	You feel	Leading to
'I really missed out there, but I'll be ready for him next time. I'll show him.'	Faulty	Frustration, anger	Future aggression
'There's no need for him to be so abrasive. Still, he's the boss and I don't suppose there's much I can do about the way he behaves.'	Faulty	Helplessness, self pity, or hurt	Future nonassertion
'I needn't have been so cowed even if he is the boss. Next time he is aggressive I can stand up to him.'	Sound	Concern, some confidence	Future assertion

In order to help you get on board with a sound inner dialogue we would like to say a bit more about other people's emotional overtones that accompany their aggression. (You may recall that in Chapter 8 we said these emotional overtones hook your own negative feelings, leading you to behave aggressively or nonassertively.) Two of the feelings that often lie behind people's aggression are anger and frustration. These are feelings that many people never learn to deal with effectively. They learn to suppress them or to give vent to them, and this latter sometimes means projecting them on to other people.

So when a person expresses anger against you he may well be angry with *himself*, in fact, but instead he projects it on to *you*. He might say things like 'You make me furious when you don't follow the laid down procedure'; whereas he is actually frustrated at himself because he has not succeeded in coming up with a procedure that works and is easy to follow. At other times people may feel angry with *someone else* whom they cannot express their anger to; if you happen to be around at the time they may take this anger out on you.

If you have developed a sound inner dialogue and productive feelings, you have overcome two barriers to making changes in the way you handle aggression from others. Also, these inner dialogues will help you to trigger off sound inner dialogues *during* an aggressive attack from someone. We refer to these later in the next section. Let us now look at ways of maintaining your assertion in the face of aggression.

Responding assertively to aggression from others

The aim in handling other people's aggression is *to get the interaction on to an assertive–assertive exchange, so that the issues are dealt with and you feel good about the interaction afterwards.* In addition, handling aggression with assertion reduces the chances of aggression recurring from that person in future.

A MODEL FOR HANDLING AGGRESSION FROM OTHERS

In Figure 9.1 we introduce a model for maintaining your assertion in the face of other people's aggression. The specific aim of this model is to *defuse the aggression* in the other person as soon as possible.

The model consists of a number of steps you can use to hold your ground in the face of aggression. The first step is different from the others. It involves having a split-second sound inner dialogue, as the person launches into her attack. The other steps are related to the various types of assertion we introduced in Chapter 5.

EXAMPLES OF THE MODEL AT WORK

We give some examples in Table 9.1 of Step 1—the split-second inner dialogue you might have (together with the accompanying feelings and resultant behaviour). Naturally, we encourage you to make this a *sound* dialogue, so that the feelings will be more productive and the behaviour assertive.

We will go on now and illustrate the rest of the model at work, starting from Step 2. We start by showing how an aggressive attack developed when the model was *not* used. This example is the beginning of a telephone conversation between David (the manager) and George (one of his staff).

DAVID: 'You've really landed me in it this time, haven't you?'
GEORGE: 'What the hell are you talking about?'

105

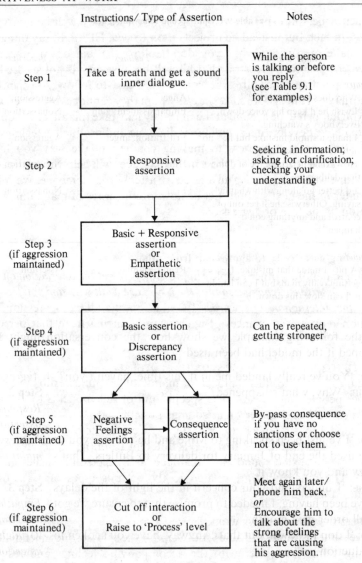

Figure 9.1 Model for handling aggression from others

DAVID: 'You know perfectly well what I'm talking about.'

GEORGE: 'I wouldn't be asking if I knew would I?'

DAVID: 'I've just been speaking to Mike and he tells me you promised the end of January for delivery to Butlers. That's crazy and you know it.'

GEORGE: 'It's no crazier than some of the promises you've been making.'

etc.

Table 9.1. Split-second inner dialogues

Inner dialogue	Feelings	Behaviour
Faulty		
– 'Who does he think he is?'	Anger	Aggression
– 'I wish he'd keep his voice down. Everybody's watching.'	Embarrassment; guilt	Nonassertion
– 'I made a stupid mistake but he's no right to go on like this.'	Frustration; anger	Aggression
– 'How could he accuse me of doing that deliberately?'	Hurt	Nonassertion
– 'I'd better go along with what he's saying. Otherwise he'll get out of control and anything could happen.'	Fear	Nonassertion
Sound		
– 'A pity I made that mistake. He's getting really mad, but I can handle it. I can slow this down.'	Regret; calmness	Assertion

In the following example we show how the conversation might have developed if the model had been used.

DAVID: 'You've really landed me in it this time, haven't you?' *Aggression*
GEORGE: 'Why, what's happened?' **Step 2** *Responsive assertion*

DAVID: 'I've just been speaking to Mike and he tells me you've promised the end of January for delivery to Butlers. That's crazy and you know it.' *Aggression maintained*

GEORGE: 'I understand your concern in the light of the delays we've been having. I needed to promise that to ensure we got a full order next month.' **Step 3** *Empathetic assertion*

DAVID: 'I don't know about that. Anyway, have you spoken to production yet?' *'Grudging' assertion*

In this example George's use of responsive assertion (Step 2) did not lead to an assertive response from David. However, by seeking information, he quickly becomes clearer on the facts and is able to respond to them. His empathetic assertion in Step 3 brings what we call a 'grudging assertion' from David.

The next example is where the aggression is maintained for much longer, and does not become assertion until after a consequence assertion has been used at Step 5. The situation is where Peter is in a meeting, when a colleague, John, makes a personal attack upon him. John says:

'That's typical of the way your department has ignored our requests since *you* took over.'

We concentrate on Peter's possible responses (starting with Step 2 of the model) in the face of John's continued aggression:

PETER		JOHN
Step 2 Responsive	'What makes you say that, John?'	
		Aggression maintained
Step 3 Basic and responsive	I don't believe we have ignored your requests, John, but I'd like to hear why you feel we have.'	
Empathetic	'I recognize your strong feelings on this, John, but I don't agree with the statement you've just made.'	
		Aggression maintained
Step 4 Basic	'I don't agree with the statement you've just made, John.'	
	or	
Discrepancy	'On the one hand you say you want to improve relations between our departments, but on the other you make statements that don't fit in with the facts as I see them.'	
		Aggression maintained
Step 5 Negative feelings	'John, I feel very annoyed when you make statements like the one earlier. They make it more difficult for me to get my staff to make the effort required to meet your requests. I'd like you to recognize the efforts they do make.'	
	or	
Consequence	'John, if you continue to make attacks upon my department's efforts, I will start to treat your requests strictly according to the book.'	
		'Grudging' assertion

NOTES ON THE STEPS OF THE MODEL

The following notes include explanations and some examples for the different steps of the model.

Step 2

Aggression often comes to you as a bolt from the blue, for example when someone rings you up or bursts into your office. When this occurs it is crucial to be clear what the other person is saying and why he is saying it. Particularly where someone is extremely aggressive, the words often come out very quickly and may not even be coherent to you. Responsive assertions in the form of those listed below are necessary to reach the point where you have enough information to be able to respond assertively to the point being made.

Seeking	'When did this happen, John?'
information	'Why do you say that, Steve?'
	'What's actually happened?'
	'Can you give me some specific examples, Dave?'
Asking for	'What do you mean by . . .?'
clarification	'When you say . . ., what were you thinking of?'
Checking your	'So have I got it right; What you're saying is . . .?'
understanding	'Can I just check that what you're saying is . . .?'

It is crucial, of course, that you ask these questions assertively, in particular keeping your voice up and evenly paced. Slowing your response down may encourage the other person to slow down and to start giving you some facts to work on. Asking questions, and listening to the responses, shows the aggressor that you are open-minded at this stage. Allowing the other person to talk also helps him to relax slightly. Sometimes he may be so pent-up that you are unable to get a word in even to ask a question. In this case it is often better to let him get it off his chest. Once this has happened the exchange stands a better chance of becoming an assertive–assertive one.

If this does not happen and the other person maintains his aggression in response to your questions, then you can move up to Step 3 of the model.

Step 3

At this stage you are saying more about *where you stand* on the issue under discussion. At the same time, both options (basic, and responsive or empathetic) show you are interested in the other person's position. The aggressor may well feel at this stage that he is getting through to you, even if your assertion shows him that your position is still different from his. This does not necessarily stop him trying to influence you, but it does make it more likely that he will now feel able to try and influence you through what he has to *say*, rather than the *way he says it*. If this happens, his behaviour will become more assertive and less aggressive.

The behaviours in Steps 2 and 3 do form a powerful combination. It is often more difficult for people to go on being aggressive to someone who is being assertive in this way. But why not test this out for yourself? Read the previous example and see how difficult you find it to maintain your aggression in the light of the assertive statements in Steps 2 and 3.

Step 4

You step up your assertion at this stage if the other person maintains his aggression in spite of your efforts at Steps 2 and 3. Here you increase the emphasis upon *your position*.

The first option is a basic assertion on its own. This may be a restatement of your position, or it may be different from earlier statements in that it takes account of new information contained in the other person's most recent contribution. In order to give strength to a restatement of your position it is useful to slow it down and give emphasis to key words. So in the following example (taken from Step 4 of the Peter and John exchange) you would emphasize the words in italics: 'I *don't agree* with the *statement* you've just *made*, John.'

In addition, following another aggressive response from the other person, you could choose before going on to Step 5 to restate your position *yet again*. This time your basic assertion would be even slower and probably shorter, with greater emphasis on key words. For instance, 'I *don't agree* with your *statement*' or 'I *don't agree*, John.'

Your other alternative is to use discrepancy assertion if appropriate. Using basic assertion as suggested above or discrepancy assertion may move the other person to assertion. If not, you move to Step 5.

Step 5

Here you can choose to work through both negative feelings assertion and consequence, or to use just one of them. Most people at this stage realize that you mean business, and may as a result move to a 'grudging' assertion. By this we mean the sort of behaviour that starts off with phrases like 'Well, all right, then' or 'OK, but . . .'. A useful consequence assertion, when dealing with aggression, is to say that you will end the interaction unless the other person changes his behaviour: 'Ron, if you continue to shout in this way, I shall put the phone down, and ring you back later. I'd prefer to sort the problem out now,' As with all consequence assertions, it is crucial to say it in a matter of fact way.

Step 6

If all your efforts so far have failed, you might be saying to yourself 'Well, that's it. I've tried everything else, now I can be aggressive without feeling bad about it!' Before your faulty dialogue leads you into aggression, there are two more options open to you.

One is to cut off the interaction. You may already have warned him of this in the previous step (as we illustrated with the consequence assertion above). But in any case a simple statement along the following lines will be sufficient at this point: 'I don't feel that we are making progress. I'd like us to meet tomorrow when we have had time to think about the problem'; or 'I am not prepared to continue in this way. Let's . . .'.

Using negative feelings or consequence assertion, or cutting off your interaction in this way, alerts the other person to the effect of her behaviour. She may not have thought too much about this before. Also, these options make it clear that you are not prepared to take her maintained aggression.

The second option is what we call 'raising to the process level'. This is particularly useful when similar incidents keep recurring. What you do is to put aside the issue you are discussing (or arguing about!) and encourage the other person to talk about the underlying issue or feelings that are leading him to behave aggressively towards you. An example of this is the difficulties Andy (the manager) was having with one of his staff (Gordon). Andy had been doing his present job for about three months. During this time, he had found Gordon very aggressive towards him. The issues they disagreed over did not seem that important as far as Andy could see, but Gordon appeared very reluctant to move an inch even when Andy made it clear he was prepared to compromise. Andy thought that Gordon had strong feelings of resentment towards him and that it was probably because he got the job rather than Gordon. Andy decided to raise this the next time Gordon got locked into a lengthy aggressive exchange. So, after arguing over a particular procedure for about 20 minutes, Andy said: 'Gordon, over the last three months we have spent a lot of time arguing over various issues. I'd like to be clearer why this has happened. Can we forget the procedure for the moment and talk about why we have these long arguments?'

Such an approach can be successful in that Gordon may start talking about his underlying feelings. If he does, Andy will become clearer on what these feelings are, and Gordon may move towards recognizing and acknowledging them. This opens the door to their improving the relationship in the future.

This approach does not always work, because the other person may refuse to talk on this level. In addition, the assertive person needs a lot of skill in listening and questioning. So we recommend that you use this approach only if all else has failed and if you feel reasonably confident of handling such a situation.

NOTES ON USING THE MODEL

1. Use the model as guidelines, not as a rigid set of rules to be followed. Thus, you may have to use several similar behaviours during one particular step.

(For instance, at Step 2 you may need to ask several questions to get a clear picture of the issue involved, and examples related to it.) In other cases you might omit a step (for instance, coming in at Step 3 if you are clear on what the person is saying).

2. Move up to the next step on the model only if the aggression is maintained. Otherwise your increased assertion may cause his aggression to increase. We have found that in many situations we can convert aggression into assertion without using the higher levels of assertion. The knowledge that we have the higher-level options should we need them increases our ability to behave very firmly when using the lower-level assertions.

3. Move your assertion down to lower-level assertion if the person becomes assertive or less aggressive.

CAN THE MODEL BE USED WITH HIGHLY AGGRESSIVE PEOPLE?
The model provides you with guidelines for handling what could otherwise become quite lengthy aggressive exchanges from others. It works in most situations and with most people. *It may not work with a small number of people.* These are the people with whom it is seemingly impossible to interact on an assertive–assertive basis. This may be because their aggression is so entrenched they find it extremely difficult to move away from it for any length of time; or it may be because you may not feel prepared to move to the higher levels of assertion to handle their aggression (for instance, with a very senior manager).

Whatever the reason, we believe the secret is to 'cut your losses', so to speak. By this we mean, learn to live with them (at least until you have become skilled at handling aggression) and meanwhile use your energy in more productive ways.

'Learning to live with' these highly aggressive people involves two things:

1. Still maintaining your own assertion in the face of the aggression, but in a less 'ambitious' way—where you are not using the higher levels of assertion to defuse the other person's aggression

2. Converting a faulty dialogue into a sound one. So, for instance:
'It's awful that Ron is so aggressive but there's nothing I can do   *Faulty*
to stop him.'   *dialogue*

This faulty dialogue not only pushes you into nonassertion but also probably leads you to spend a lot of time and energy complaining to others about him and wishing he was different. It can become:

'It would be better if Ron weren't so aggressive, but he is. That's   *Sound*
really a problem for him to sort out. I don't have to let it take up   *dialogue*
lots of my time and energy. I can at least behave assertively with

him. I may not change his aggression, but I can feel OK about
myself afterwards.'

Coping with 'everyday put-downs'

The model that we introduced above is suitable for handling not only the long,
very aggressive exchanges you face from time to time, but also the short,
one-off, low-level instances of aggression that occur more frequently. By these
we mean comments or questions like:
– 'That's personnel for you.'
– 'Haven't you finished that memo yet?'
We use the phrase 'everyday put-downs' to describe these examples of
low-level aggression. They come in all shapes and sizes and are aimed at
putting you in a 'one-down' position. They form part of life's niggles, and
unless you cope with them, they can eat away at you, and sour your
relationship with the person who makes them.

One way you may handle them at the moment is to notice them but let them
pass (n.a.). Another way is to respond in kind, hopefully finding a 'clever'
retort (agg). Both of these may encourage the other person to keep the
'put-downs' going, either because he sees he can make them with impunity or
because he enjoys 'niggling' you or making you feel uncomfortable.

Next time you are on the receiving end of a put-down, we suggest you
respond assertively to it. As it is a low-level aggression it will be appropriate to
use Steps 2 and 3 of the model—responsive, basic-plus-responsive, or
empathetic assertions. In the following section we describe an exercise for
practising these sort of responses to the put-downs you encounter.

EXERCISE FOR COPING WITH PUT-DOWNS

Part One
In Table 9.2 we have listed examples of some of the more common types of
put-downs (but the list is not exhaustive). We suggest you use the list in the
following way.

1. Modify the list of examples in any way you like until it corresponds to
   put-downs that you have encountered in the past.
2. Produce a form of words that you feel happy to use as an assertive response
   to each of the put-downs. (Remember to use basic, responsive or
   empathetic assertions.)
3. Compare your responses with the ones we have suggested in Table 9.3. If
   they are different it does not mean they are wrong, as there are several
   different assertive responses you can make to each put-down. The
   important thing is that a response should be assertive in *stating your*

113

position and in *showing that you will not let the put-down succeed.* This will decrease the chances of that person making such a put-down in the future.

Table 9.2. Exercise: Coping with everyday put-downs

Type of put-down	Example	Your assertive response
Stereotyping you	'That's typical of the way all you accountants think.'	
Insinuating	'I expect you've got plenty of spare time in your department.'	
Making decisions on your behalf	'What I'd do, if I were you, is spend less time on the detail of your job.'	
Questioning your judgement, values, or beliefs	'Are you really sure he'll be able to do the job?' 'You don't really believe *that*, do you?'	
Patronizing	'Well don't worry yourself about all that. I'll take care of it.'	
Nagging	'How much longer are you going to spend on that report?'	
Inferring you are lying	'Oh, come on, you know that's not how it happened.'	
Making generalizations about your personality	'I think you're far too nice to succeed.'	
Using emotive words to describe your actions	'That was a crazy decision.' 'It was irresponsible of you not to let me know.'	

Table 9.3. Possible answers to the put-downs

Example put-down	Possible assertive reply
'That's typical of the way all you accountants think.'	'I don't believe it's typical. It's only the way I'm thinking about *this* issue.'
'I expect you've got plenty of spare time in your department.'	'What makes you say that?'

Table 9.3 *(continued)*

Example put-down	*Possible assertive reply*
'What I'd do, if I were you, is spend less time on the detail of your job.'	'I appreciate your concern, John, but I'd like to make that decision for myself.'
'Are you really sure, he'll be able to do the job?'	'I believe he will.'
'You don't really believe *that*, do you?'	'Yes, I do believe that.'
'Well, don't worry yourself about all that. I'll take care of it.'	'I'm not worried about it, but I am concerned. I'm happy to look after it myself.'
'How much longer are you going to spend on that report?'	'Why are you asking?' 'I recognize that you're keen to have it. However, I shall probably need to spend two more days on it.'
'Oh come on, you know that's not how it happened.'	'That certainly is the way I saw it.'
'I think you're far too nice to succeed.'	'I don't see it that way.' 'I don't agree with you. I think I'll succeed if I want to.'
'That was a crazy decision.'	'I'm not happy with the decision in retrospect, but I don't think it was crazy.'
'It was irresponsible of you not to let me know.'	'I accept that it was a mistake not to let you know, but I would not describe it as irresponsible.'

Part Two

We now suggest you practise making your responses in an assertive way. You can do this on your own, although you will probably have more fun and learn more if you invite someone to join you. Your 'partner' does not have to know much about assertiveness as long as he can make the put-downs to you in the mildly aggressive manner you are familiar with. If you are working with someone else you need to give him the list of examples and ask him to say the put-downs to you in *random* order. You then respond with the words you decided on in Part One, or with similar ones. If you are on your own, just practise saying the responses out loud to yourself. (It's OK to talk to yourself!) Either way, take your time in saying your responses. Because the put-downs often come rapidly, 'out of the blue', you may think you have to react and respond quickly. But this can actually make your assertion less effective.

115

Conclusion

Having carried out the 'coping with everyday put-downs' exercise and feeling satisfied with the way you responded to the put-downs, you are now in a position to make these responses the next time these put-downs are made for real.

When you are dealing with more sustained, or higher-level aggression, the model introduced earlier in the chapter will be useful to you.

10. Handling nonassertion from others

In Chapter 8 we said that nonassertion from other people can influence your own behaviour. We explained how the emotions accompanying the other person's nonassertion hook your own feelings, which in turn can move you away from assertion into nonassertion or aggression, depending on which feelings you have. In addition, we said that you may change your mind—about a decision, an opinion, or a course of action—not so much because you are responding to the content of what the person says, but because you are responding to the nonassertive behaviour itself. Whether the nonassertion influences you to change your mind or not, the other person still gets something of what he wants. He may have led you to feel sorry or guilty on his behalf, which can be comforting and rewarding to him. Or he may have aroused your anger, irritation, or frustration, which in turn will lead him to feel hurt or self-pity, both of which can be comforting to him and thus reinforcing. All this 'emotional blackmail' is not only pretty unhealthy, but it also makes it difficult for you to have open, straightforward dealings with a person behaving nonassertively.

In a sense there is a temptation to leave people to their own devices when they behave nonassertively—because they are not necessarily violating your rights, as people are when they behave aggressively. If nonassertion had *no* effect on you, then this would certainly be one way of handling it. But as we have already said, nonassertion affects your own feelings and behaviour, and can affect the outcome of a situation (we give more examples of this later in the chapter). In addition, the definition of assertiveness includes 'not violating the rights, not ignoring the needs, wants and opinions of others'. So in order for you to be assertive, you need *to know* what these needs, wants and opinions are—sometimes difficult when people are nonassertive about expressing them!

Therefore, in this chapter we look at how to handle nonassertion assertively, so that you retain control over your own feelings and behaviour while also moving the other person some way towards behaving more assertively in return. We explore different forms of nonassertion and some ways of responding assertively to them.

Different forms of nonassertion

In Table 10.1 we look more closely at some of the different forms of nonassertion that you may come into contact with at work. (Some of these we have mentioned in earlier chapters.)

Table 10.1. A closer look at forms of nonassertion

Form of N.A.	Examples	What might really be going on?
Tentative or reluctant agreement	'Oh, I suppose so.' 'Well it might be OK.' 'Maybe you're right.'	Going along with you because they are unwilling to disagree; wanting to avoid conflict; wanting to please you.
Hinting at or tentatively expressing doubts/difficulties	'I'm not really sure about that.' 'That may be a bit awkward.'	Playing 'safe'. They can then retract the doubt if you get aggressive; or if you behave nonassertively they can then state the doubt in 'safety'.
Stating excuses	'I haven't really got time.' 'I would, only I'm rushed off my feet.' 'I can't really because I have to. . .'	'Time' and 'overwork' are the more common 'smokescreens'. They are putting you off the 'scent' of the real reason, which may be an unstated preference or a lack of ability and/or confidence.
Unwilling to state preferences	'Oh, I don't really mind.' 'Whichever way suits you best.'	Wanting to be helpful or sometimes unwilling to take responsibility. Often have preferences but unwilling to state them—may prefer to complain afterwards.
Moaning or complaining —about you	'Oh dear, not another set of figures.' 'Oh no! We've got so much to do.'	Maybe to you directly or just within earshot—trying to make you feel guilty.
—about a third party	'They expect you to do everything all at once.'	Trying to enlist your support. Often unwilling to take direct action—prefer your sympathy instead.
Eliciting approval	'I thought it didn't go too well, what do you think?'	Often don't believe this negative self-assessment, but want you not only to disagree with it but probably to be complimentary.

Table 10.1 *(continued)*

Form of N.A.	Examples	What might really be going on?
Eliciting confirmation/permission	'I thought I might . . . do you think I should?'	Unwilling to base decisions on their own judgement—often about matters that do not affect you. They have your advice to back them up if anything goes wrong. (Not the same as collecting facts about how things might work out, or seeking your reaction to things that affect you.)
Helplessness and self pity	'I don't think I'll ever get this lot sorted out. I don't seem to be getting anywhere.' 'What's the use of . . .'	Seeing themselves as powerless to influence their surroundings/make changes in their own behaviour. Wanting you to feel sorry for their 'plight'. Sometimes to avoid taking action.
Self put-downs	'I'm hopeless at maths.' 'You know me, I'm bound to get it all wrong.' 'I made a real mess of that presentation.'	There may be a genuine lack of ability and/or confidence, but often expressed as exaggerations, understating capabilities—sometimes to avoid doing something or to avoid criticism (by getting in first); sometimes to elicit a compliment.
Proposals at their own expense	'Would you like me to take that home? I really don't mind.' 'I haven't a lot of time but I can do it in the lunch break.'	Over-helpfulness. Often trying to please you. Sometimes trying to put you in their debt so you'll feel grateful. Sometimes wanting you to feel guilty about them going out of their way in denying their own needs and wants.
Enhancing others at their own expense	'You always seem to get on well using these machines. I'm hopeless at it.' 'She's so calm about handling awkward customers. There's no way I could be like that.'	Wanting to admire or flatter the other person. Negative comparisons sometimes enable the person to avoid criticism or taking on a new or difficult task.

ANOTHER FORM OF NONASSERTION

In the examples in Table 10.1 the nonassertion consists of statements that are tentative, apologetic, or self-demeaning. A rather different, but very common,

119

form of nonassertion is when a person *fails to say anything at all.* Examples of this would be failing to raise an important issue, to state disagreement, or to state wants. When a person keeps quiet like this it may not affect you at the time, but it can often rebound on you later on. For instance, has the following sort of thing ever happened to you? You were in a meeting where people agreed to submit monthly progress reports. Three of your colleagues clearly supported this idea while a fourth *did not disagree.* At the end of the month four of you produced reports as agreed, but your remaining colleague did not. When you asked him about this you discovered he did not think it was a good idea in the first place!

This form of nonassertion is difficult to detect at the time. However, there may well be some nonverbal clues that can help you to spot this 'silent' nonassertion. Here are some examples:

Lack of eye contact—maybe even 'shifty' sidelong glances
Facial expressions—face puckering or lips pursed indicating doubt
Shuffling body movements ⎫ indicating a wish to get away, to avoid
Restless hand movements ⎭ potential disagreement

The pattern that emerges with many of these forms of nonassertion is that you are unclear on what the other person really believes, feels, or wants. You may even end up not trusting him; you suspect he says one thing but does another—a particularly effective form of sabotage against you. With all the forms of nonassertion, the person may or may not be aware of his behaviour and its effects on you. What matters though is that *you* are now aware of what *might* be going on. So you are in a better position to handle some of the exchanges you get involved in, some of which might otherwise be quite lengthy and unproductive.

Responding assertively to nonassertion

The aim, when you are responding assertively to nonassertion, is to get the interaction on to an ass–ass level. This involves you in retaining control over yourself, first of all.

RETAINING CONTROL OF YOUR FEELINGS
The first step towards this is being *aware* of how the other person's nonassertion can influence your own feelings.

The second step is to have a *sound inner dialogue* with yourself, as follows:

1. If you know *in advance* that you are going to meet with a person who is often nonassertive, you can 'talk to yourself' beforehand. For example:
   'I know Dave is usually over-helpful, making promises he cannot keep. I can get him to be realistic and to state any problems. I need not be fobbed off by unrealistic promises.'
2. If a person has come to you *unexpectedly* and you find yourself having to

respond to his nonassertion, then you can take a deep breath and hold a split second inner dialogue. For example:

'Bob seems to be giving me excuses. I need not let that irritate me. I can get at the real reason.'

BEHAVING ASSERTIVELY IN THE FACE OF NONASSERTION

In Table 10.2 we give some examples of assertive responses to six nonassertive replies. The aim with all of the assertive responses is to get at the issues and avoid the emotional blackmail of the nonassertion; then, having done this, to get the other person to behave assertively in return. The nonassertions are six of the many possible replies that a person could give in the following situation.

Situation: You have previously mentioned to a subordinate that when his project finishes you would need a report from him within a month of the finish date. The project has now ended, so you want to agree a deadline for the report. You say 'Bill, you know that project report I mentioned, I'd like to have it from you by the end of the month. Is that OK with you?'

Table 10.2. Examples of assertive responses to nonassertion

N.A. reply	Ass. response	Comments
1. 'Well . . . all right, then.' (*tentative agreement*)	'You seem to be hesitating. Do you see a difficulty?' (*responsive*)	Can you be sure the report will be ready? You need to find out if there *is* a problem before you can get a firm commitment.
'That . . . er . . . may leave me with a bit of a problem.' (*tentatively expressing doubts*)	'What is the problem? Let's see if it can be sorted out.' (*responsive and/or basic*)	This makes it clear that you realize there may be a genuine problem but that it need not get in the way.
3. 'Well, I don't seem to be able to find time to get started on it.' (*stating excuses*)	'Oh, I see. Well, I think there may be a way round that. But is that the only problem, Bill, or is there something else?' (*basic or empathetic and responsive*)	Sometimes difficult to distinguish an excuse from a real reason. This response avoids 'red rag' words (like 'excuses' or 'real') that may make him think you are accusing him of lying.
4. 'I haven't a lot of time as I'm out this week and next, but I suppose I can work at home over the weekend'. (*proposals at own expense*)	'I'm glad you mentioned about being out this week and next. But can we look for ways around this so you don't have to work over the weekend?' (*empathetic or basic+responsive*)	This enables you to avoid feeling guilty, sorry, or over-grateful. If there is no way around this and you have to accept the offer simply say 'Thank you, Bill' with no lengthy apologies.

121

Table 10.2 *(continued)*

	N.A. reply	Ass. response	Comments
5.	'I'm hopeless at writing reports. I made a real mess of the last one.' *(putting self down)*	'I wouldn't say you are hopeless at reports. The last one was not good, but I believe you *can* write reports. What specific problems do you have with them?' *(basic and responsive)*	Important to counter his exaggerations with a more realistic assessment—no effusive praise. Then give assurance to improve confidence—avoid fatherly 'pep' talks ('You'll be all right, no need to worry'). Treating him like a child encourages nonassertion.
6.	'You're very good at writing reports. I seem to find it really slow and time consuming' *(enhancing others at own expense)*	'Why do you think you find it slow and time-consuming?' *(responsive)* or 'I feel uneasy when you compare yourself unfavourably to me, like that, Bill. I'd like us to look at why you find it slow and time-consuming.' *(negative feelings)*	This does not take any note of the negative comparison but looks for facts behind the emotion. or This response is particularly useful when the other person continually uses this form of nonassertion. It starts to make him aware of his n.a. and the effects it has on you.

Of course, it is sometimes unrealistic to try and get the other person to behave assertively. If you manage to maintain your own assertion and to get him to deal with the issues *less* nonassertively, then this may be as much as you can achieve.

Sometimes the other person may get irritated and behave aggressively. So in the situation on which Table 10.2 is based, after several assertions from you he might say, 'Well, I've already told you, leave it with me.' This can happen because he realizes after a number of assertions from you that you are not playing the game he wants (feeling guilty or sorry for him). Sometimes it can be that he sees a threat in being asked several questions (asking them in matter of fact, non-criticizing ways helps to avoid this). If the person does become aggressive, then you can still stick to your assertiveness. Remember, '*you have the right to behave assertively*'. We suggest a simple basic assertion or an empathetic assertion at this stage. The following examples are in response to the above aggression, and would be said very slowly and steadily:

Basic   'Fine, Bill. But it is important for me to have a date agreed.'
Empathetic 'I recognize that you have agreed to do the report, Bill, but I do
             need to agree a definite date with you.'

A switch from nonassertion to aggression is the 'worst' that can happen to
you. In many cases you are just going to be dealing with nonassertion. In itself
this can be quite tiring, because in a sense the ball keeps coming back to you, so
that you have to keep taking the initiative.

Summary

So in this chapter we have:
– Looked at the different forms of nonassertion
– Suggested some assertive responses you can make to them
– Stressed that, although it is tempting to 'let sleeping dogs lie', this is
  undesirable because nonassertion from others leaves you with a number of
  problems—not least that it makes it more difficult for you to behave
  assertively.

11. Resolving conflict

We will assume that you are now acting more assertively yourself, and in turn are handling aggression and nonassertion from other people so that they too behave more assertively. It follows from this increase in assertiveness that more needs, wants, and preferences will be brought out into the open. Clearly, some of these needs will not only be different but may even be in conflict, at least on the surface. It may appear, therefore, that your increased assertion has left you with a problem: how to handle these conflicting needs.

In a sense, these conflicting needs were there all the time. What assertion has done is to bring them more into the open. In fact, this makes them easier to deal with. Otherwise you would be trying to deduce what they are from what people say and do (or do *not* say and do!).

This chapter helps you to handle conflicting needs in ways that are acceptable to both parties.

We will start by clarifying the different types of needs.

Types of needs

Let us assume for the moment that you are aware of the other person's needs and that he is aware of yours. Looking at the two sets of needs, it is possible to classify them into three types.

NEEDS THAT DO NOT IMPACT

Let us suppose you have said to a colleague: 'Jane, can we sort out that design problem now rather than after lunch? I need to be away early.' She may say: 'Fine, it doesn't make any difference to me whether it's this morning or this afternoon.' In other words, she does not see your suggestion and needs as affecting any of her needs at that time. In such cases, we say that the needs *do not impact*. Another example would be your asking a member of staff for a report by next Friday, and he replies: 'No problem. I'll be finishing it by Wednesday at the latest.'

Many of the everyday interactions that take place, with no hassles, are examples where the needs of the different people involved do not impact. When this happens you have no problem in accommodating both sets of needs.

NEEDS THAT ARE COMPLEMENTARY

It is possible that when you ask Jane about moving your meeting to the morning she readily agrees because the change fits in very nicely with a need she has. She wants to see her manager about some new schedules, and later

124

that afternoon is one of the few times he is free to see her. In this case, your need to be away early actually helps Jane to meet one of her needs. When this happens we say the needs *are complementary*.

Here is another example. You are looking for an additional person to join your project team for about three months. Malcolm has just finished a project of his own, he has the experience you require, and he wants to gain the further experience that your project will give him. Your need for a person with certain experience complements his need to gain further experience. When needs are complementary, again there is no problem in meeting them.

NEEDS THAT CONFLICT

Returning to our original example, Jane may not agree to your suggestion because she has committed the rest of the morning to another task that has to be finished by lunchtime. In this case, your need to sort out the design problem and be away early conflicts with her need to sort out her other task by lunchtime. On the surface, you can meet your need only at the expense of her meeting her need, or vice versa. In such situations we describe the needs as *conflicting*. Another example occurs if both you and your deputy want your holidays during the last two weeks in August, and it is not practical for you both to be away at the same time. When needs are in conflict, there is a problem in meeting them.

Now, it is inevitable that in any organization there will be examples of conflicting needs. This is not undesirable in itself. What is undesirable is that these conflicting needs should result in hostility or resentment. This happens so often because of *the way the conflict of needs is handled*.

The next section looks at some of the different ways of handling conflict that are available to you, and considers briefly some of the findings on how effective these are.

Ways of handling conflict

The behavioural exchange you and another person can have when trying to resolve conflict between you can be any of the following:

$$agg \longleftrightarrow agg$$
$$agg \longleftrightarrow n.a.$$
$$n.a. \longleftrightarrow n.a.$$
$$ass \longleftrightarrow ass$$

We will look at each of these in more detail.

AGGRESSIVE–AGGRESSIVE EXCHANGE

When needs are in conflict the exchange is often aggressive–aggressive. This arises because *each* person sees the situation as 'I win/you lose'. In other

125

words, each believes that the only way he can win is if the other person loses. Because *both* people believe this, the exchange is often lengthy and draining. A very high proportion of them end in stalemate with no solutions agreed to cope with the conflicting needs. Even where solutions are agreed, there is little chance they will be high-quality as measured by the extent to which they meet both sets of needs. This is not surprising, because much of the energy of the people involved in such exchanges goes into *beating the other person as opposed to beating the problem*. As we put it in Chapter 8, the *content* gets lost and the *behaviour* takes over.

An underlying theme to many of these interactions is the refusal of one or both parties to accept the needs of the other as legitimate. We will explore this issue in greater depth later on.

AGGRESSIVE–NONASSERTIVE EXCHANGE

Exchanges may fall into this pattern, for example, where there is a conflict of needs between a manager and a member of staff. The manager sees his needs to be more important than the other's because he is higher in the organization. The member of staff frequently supports this view because he is out to please the other. When the other is also the manager, the subordinate sees it as 'only right and fair' that the needs of the manager should be met. They *both* view the situation, therefore, as one in which the manager wins, the subordinate loses.

Because of these views there is no need for the manager to use what we have called the higher levels of aggression. He just makes statements like 'I'd be happy for you to take your holidays in August. But that's when I'm taking mine and obviously we can't both be away at the same time.' On the surface such statements appear very reasonable. However, this unquestioning acceptance by both parties of the priority needs of the manager ensures that no energy goes into seeing if there is a way of meeting both sets of needs.

Thus, the solutions emerging from these interactions are often mundane in themselves and low-quality in terms of meeting both sets of needs. The solutions are often arrived at by reference to the past. So managers and staff regularly handling conflicting needs in this way reinforce rather stereotype behaviour in each other.

Agg–n.a. exchanges have the advantage of being shorter than agg–agg or n.a.–n.a. ones. At the time they appear to be satisfactory, but later on they often come unstuck. This is because the nonassertive person held back on his doubts or disagreement and denied his needs at the time, but later feels resentment. Going back to the previous example, resentment may build up in the member of staff till he feels sufficiently aggrieved to challenge the manager's decision on a later issue. Unfortunately by this time his prior nonassertion leads him to do this aggressively rather than assertively. So he behaves as though his needs should now have priority over the manager's. They both still view the situation as a win/lose, the only difference now being

126

that the manager looks like becoming the loser! His reaction to such a prospect is to respond aggressively to stave off what he sees as a threat to his authority. The exchange may become an aggressive–aggressive one at this point.

NONASSERTIVE–NONASSERTIVE EXCHANGE

We see this as a less common exchange in the world of work, but by no means unknown among colleagues and others on the same level within an organization. It is quite common in social life, in situations where people are keen to avoid any unpleasantness and to please each other.

Strangely enough, n.a.–n.a. exchanges are similar to agg–agg ones in three ways. They tend to be long, drawn out affairs; they frequently end in stalemate; and the quality of any solutions is likely to be low. This is because each views the situation as 'I lose/you win'. This is to say, each person is wanting the other person to win; each believes that he himself has to lose in order for the other person to win. When *both* parties are operating from this basis the outcome is often what we refer to as a 'lose/lose', in that the solutions meet *neither set of needs*. They are arrived at by judging them against the criteria of how much they inconvenience, upset, or please the other person. So n.a.–n.a. exchanges are characterized by phrases like:
– 'That wouldn't be fair on you.'
– 'No I couldn't let you do that.'
– 'That will mean you having to . . . You can't possibly do that.'

ASSERTIVE–ASSERTIVE EXCHANGE

People involved in these interactions view them as 'I win/you win'. In other words, it does not mean that one person has to lose in order for the other to win. In ass–ass exchanges facts are paramount and the energy goes into beating the problem rather than the person. As a result, both parties are trying to come up with solutions that meet both of their needs. Because of this, the solutions are likely to stick, instead of people going away and doing something different. These interactions tend to be shorter than the agg–agg and n.a.–n.a. ones, although probably not as short as agg–n.a. ones.

There is often the additional bonus in that the solutions will resolve the problem of the conflicting needs in imaginative, new, or exciting ways that would not otherwise emerge. This does not necessarily mean that the needs of both parties are totally met, though this is what the exchange is aiming for. Sometimes, however, they are met to an extent that is *acceptable* to the people involved. This is not to be confused with what people often refer to as a 'shoddy compromise'. To us, this suggests that both parties feel unhappy about the outcome; pretty well the same as we described in the n.a.–n.a. exchange.

Thus we see an ass–ass exchange as the *effective* way of resolving the conflict of needs. However, if you are interacting with a person who is being aggressive

127

or nonassertive, then you would have to work through the steps suggested in Chapters 9 and 10 in order to get the exchange on to an ass–ass level.

Resolving conflicts in ways acceptable to both persons requires you to *go beyond* the stage of stating and standing up for your needs. If you only do this, you may still find yourselves reaching stalemate. You are more likely to come up with acceptable solutions if you go on and *follow certain steps* and *use certain behaviours*. We look at these in detail in the next section.

Guidelines for resolving conflict

In the first place, you have to *recognize* that there *may* be a conflict of needs. One of the warning signs of this is if you are having a *lengthy disagreement*, for instance about what course of action to take. When this occurs we suggest you operate the steps as outlined in Figure 11.1.

Identifying *needs*

↓

Checking for and accepting any *conflict* of needs

↓

Coming up with and agreeing on *solutions*

Figure 11.1. Steps in resolving the conflict of needs

Let us now look at these steps in more detail giving particular attention to the behaviours you need to use in each step.

1. IDENTIFYING NEEDS

The first thing to say is that people do not always talk in terms of *needs*. Instead, they often put forward *suggestions*. For instance, in the example we quoted earlier you may have said to your colleague: 'Jane, can we sort out that design problem now rather than after lunch?' Here the unstated need (to be away early) is known to you but not to Jane. The danger, when you do not state your real need but only talk in terms of suggestions, is that the other person will also react at that level—perhaps disagreeing with your suggestion. What happens then is that you either make more suggestions, or you push the original one harder (maybe pointing out the benefits). But suggestions are made only as a means of meeting needs. So, rather than battling away at the level of suggestions, it is more effective to *dig behind* them and get at the real needs that these suggestions are intended to meet. You can do this in two ways:

1. By making *your own needs* clear. In the above example you would state the needs that lie behind your original suggestion: 'I need to be away early and I need to sort out the design problem before I leave.'

2. By digging out the *needs of the other person* using the following behaviours:

Seeking information	'Why does that present a problem for you, Dave?'
	'How much time will you need for . . .?'
	'Which analysts would be acceptable to you?'
	'Why do you need to have this by Wednesday?'
Asking for clarification	'What do you mean by "outline" report?'
	'When you say "estimate", how detailed does it have to be?'
Checking your understanding	'So are you saying . . .?'
	'Have I got it right, what you're saying is . . .?'

What you are doing here is to follow up the *clues* to get at the real needs. So, for instance, when you have put forward a suggestion the conversation might go as follows:

DAVE: No. That's no good.'	*Disagreement*
YOU: Why do you say that, Dave?'	*Seeking information*
DAVE: 'It won't give me enough lead time before I have to make the actual launch.'	*Clue*
YOU: 'How much lead time do you need?'	*Following a clue (seeking information)*
DAVE: 'At least three weeks.'	*Real need*

This is not to suggest that the other person is deliberately trying to mislead you (although this may be true), but that, in order to stop yourself rushing headlong into a dispute, you need as much background information as possible about both sets of needs. You can collect this information by actually asking the other person rather than making guesses. The following are some examples of the sort of needs that might emerge:

– 'I need to finish my present survey before taking on another one.'
– 'I need to feel confident that any new scheme is practical before giving it the go-ahead.'
– 'I need my manager's agreement, and he is firmly against that sort of approach.'
– I need to get my budget down to target before agreeing any new expenditures.'
– 'I need to have it completed within a fortnight.'

Of course, in some cases people will not 'come clean' about what their real needs are. This is particularly true where these needs are of a personal nature. Examples of this would be the need to look good in the eyes of a senior manager or the need to win out over a colleague. Other people are not behaving assertively when they hold back on such needs. You may be able to sense that they have a need of this sort, if you listen carefully to their responses when you try to delve a bit deeper in a particular area. In some cases you may

129

have no indication of such needs. In either case their lack of assertion is going to make it more difficult for you to resolve the conflict to the satisfaction of both parties. At times you can minimize the risk of the other person refusing to 'come clean' by doing your 'delving' in the assertive ways we refer to in the following paragraph. But at other times you may have to be realistic in accepting that not everyone is prepared to be open with you.

When you are delving to get at real needs, with questions like 'Why do you need to . . .?' it is important that you are not at this stage seen to be questioning the validity of the need as stated. (It is legitimate to do this, but it is better left till *after* the real needs have been identified. We will go into more detail on this in the next section.) So you need to ask questions in matter-of-fact ways, not letting your voice contain tones that suggest criticism or judgement. It also helps if you can avoid evaluating or showing disbelief at the statements the other person makes, with remarks like: 'What's the good of that?' or 'What on earth for?'

2. CHECKING FOR AND ACCEPTING THE CONFLICT OF NEEDS

Having identified the real needs of both parties, you want to check whether there is any conflict between these needs. In other words, can one set of needs be met only at the expense of the other?

Sometimes you will discover that, contrary to your first impression, the needs are not in fact in conflict. Instead, you have two sets of needs that *do not impact*. This is because, as a result of delving deeper, you can begin to see that there are various options emerging for ways of meeting both sets of needs. When this happens you can go straight on to the third step of coming up with and agreeing solutions.

At other times, after identifying both sets of needs there will actually be a conflict between these needs. In this case it is useful to *summarize* the conflict as you see it: 'So it looks like we have a problem in that your need to . . . conflicts with my need to . . .'. Before you can move on to agreeing solutions it is vital that both parties then go on and accept each other's needs.

Acceptance of needs

We have noticed that, when people have conflicting sets of needs, they often have difficulty in accepting each other's needs. This barrier may arise because of a fear of losing out. The clearest indicator that one person does *not* accept the other person's need is when she puts energy into *persuading* him that he does not 'really' have this need.

At other times the barrier to accepting needs may arise because the needs are not seen as *legitimate*. In order for a need to be recognized as legitimate it must be seen to stem from an agreed right. Supposing you say to a colleague: 'I need your guarantee that you will release Mike to do this study for us next month.' Your colleague may reply: 'I cannot *guarantee* that, as our terms of

130

reference clearly state we have to give priority to requests from the factory, and we may well get some by then.' In effect, he is not recognising your need for a guarantee as being a legitimate need, because of his terms of reference.

You can uncover these barriers to acceptance and reach a mutual acceptance of each other's needs by using the following behaviours:

Stating your acceptance	'I recognize that you need to . . .'
Gaining his acceptance	'So, do you accept that I need to . . .?'

When people fail to really accept each other's needs it makes the next step of coming up with and agreeing solutions very difficult. We believe this is a major cause of conflicts taking a long time to be resolved. This sometimes happens, for example, with industrial relations disputes. The management side (to use the common description) does not really accept their employees' need to be kept informed, to be consulted, to have a reasonable degree of control over their work and the way they do it. The trade unions, in turn, do not really accept management's need to make an adequate profit, or to make changes in response to the market.

Being able to accept each other's needs, even though they are in conflict, opens the door to being able to resolve the conflict.

COMING UP WITH AND AGREEING ON SOLUTIONS

Once the needs have been accepted, this phase can be creative and rewarding. Below we list some of the behaviours that are essential in generating solutions that go a long way towards meeting the needs of both parties.

Seeking suggestions	'So how shall we get around this one?'
	'Any suggestions on how . . .?'
Making suggestions	'I think we could . . .'
	'I suggest that we . . .'
	'How about if we . . .'
Reacting	'I think that will work.'
(to suggestions)	'I don't think that will work out, Steve.'
	'I agree with the first part of your idea but not the second.'
Developing	'If we do X as you suggest, we could also go on and do Y.'
(others' suggestions)	
	'How about changing the second part of your idea to . . .?'
Seeking reactions	'Do you agree with that?'
(to your ideas)	'Will that work?'
	'How do you feel about that?'
Summarizing	'OK, so we've agreed to . . .'
	'Fine, so I'll . . . and you'll. . . .'

Let us say a few words about some of these.

Reacting to suggestions

You are being assertive when you react to suggestions to let others know whether you agree or disagree. Keeping quiet when you have doubt about a suggestion is being nonassertive; ignoring a suggestion is being aggressive. Continually pointing out the flaws in suggestions is also likely to be seen as aggressive after a time and may result in potentially useful ideas being lost. To avoid this, a more creative approach is to say what bits you like about an idea and what bits you do not like: 'I agree that we could get the other departments involved but probably not until next month.'

Developing a suggestion

This takes this positive approach of reacting to other people's suggestions a stage further. Here, when you agree with a suggestion or part of it, you extend it by adding on to it a suggestion of your own. Your own suggestion must of course complement rather than contradict the original. An example could be:

Your colleague says: 'I think we ourselves could give more time to the rings project.'

You say: 'Yes. And when we have done the groundwork we could get Mike to work on the details.'

Developing ideas and suggestions in this way can lead to high-quality solutions to problems; solutions that neither of you might have come up with on your own. When both of you are involved in this way, you are both more likely to feel committed to the solution.

Some concluding comments

This approach, because it is based upon an assertive–assertive exchange, puts the emphasis upon resolving the conflict by defeating the problem, rather than by defeating the other person. The suggestions agreed can be such that they go a long way towards meeting both parties' needs. If they do, then they will be seen as *highly acceptable* by both parties. When you are dealing with particularly difficult situations, it may be possible only to come up with suggestions that are *moderately acceptable* to you and the other person concerned. When you have used the guidelines suggested to reach this outcome, it does help both parties to recognize that this is the best solution that you can come up with for the time being. It enables you both to leave the interaction saying things to yourselves like: 'So, I didn't get all I wanted out of it. However, we came up with what I believe to be the best solution in the circumstances.'

Both types of outcomes (the highly acceptable and the moderately acceptable) are what we have called win/win. At the end of the interaction you will feel satisfied or even excited—productive feelings, which make it easier to handle future conflicts effectively.

12. Contributing assertively to meetings

To many managers, meetings are an important part of their job—not only in terms of the time they spend in them, but also because other managers make judgements upon their competence based upon their performance in meetings. You may share this view of the importance of meetings. But do you sometimes have doubts about the effectiveness of meetings, or about your own performance in them? If so, we think you will find this chapter interesting because it aims to help you become more effective in contributing to meetings.

We will concentrate on *contributing to*, rather than *running meetings* because this is the aspect that involves most people. Even when the chairman is not that skilled at running meetings, by improving your own effectiveness you can do a great deal to make sure the meeting is still effective. In addition, you will be able to adapt some of the items we mention for when you are running a meeting.

Before we go any further, let us say what we mean by a meeting. We are defining a meeting as: *when three or more people come together for at least 30 minutes to achieve a result.*

Now, the success of any meeting depends upon two major factors. For convenience we shall call them the *mechanics* and the *behaviour*. By 'mechanics' we mean such things as:

- The presence or absence of a clear objective for the meeting
- The quality of the agenda
- Whether the 'right' people are there
- Administration—members getting adequate notice, preparation and distribution of paperwork, suitable surroundings, seating arrangements, etc.

By 'behaviour' we are referring to what the members and chairman say and do before and during the meeting. *Both* factors need to be handled well if the meeting is to be successful, but because this book is about behaviour, this is the area we will look at.

We believe any meeting would benefit from more assertive behaviour from both its members and its chairman. It seems that many people find it more difficult to behave assertively in meetings than they do say in a one-to-one interaction. For instance, you may put forward your ideas, and agree or disagree, when you are interacting with just one other person; yet, in a meeting with six or seven others, you may hold back from stating your ideas, or opinions—behaving nonassertively. On the other hand, you may behave aggressively by overstating your disagreement so that it becomes an attack upon the other person.

This increase in nonassertion and aggression occurs because most people see meetings as more uncomfortable, stressful, or challenging situations than one-to-one interactions. Therefore, they have more faulty inner dialogues and are unclear on the rights they have as members. We will look at each of these in turn, and then we will give some hints for behaving more assertively in meetings.

Inner dialogues for contributing to meetings

If you believe the 'spotlight' is on you when you contribute to a meeting, then you can have some faulty dialogues before, during and after a meeting. Table 12.1 gives examples of some of the sound and faulty dialogues we have come across. Take a look at your own inner dialogue, and turn any faulty ones into

Table 12.1. Examples of inner dialogues about meetings

Faulty inner dialogues	*Equivalent sound dialogues*
Before a meeting	
1. 'I'm obviously going to be in a minority, so what is the point in saying anything?'	'I may be in a minority, but I can put over my views concisely and clearly to try and influence them. If I fail I'll be disappointed, but I'll have done as much as I can.'
2. 'I'll use the meeting to really put Mike on the spot by asking him about the new procedure.'	'If I'm angry with Mike about the new procedure, then I can raise it with him on a one-to-one without resorting to playing games at the meeting.'
During a meeting	
3. 'If I make my suggestion, other members may think it's silly and I'll look a fool.'	'I have the right to put forward my suggestion and to have it listened to. They may not agree with my suggestion, but that doesn't mean they'll think it's silly.'
4. 'I can't let Ray get away with that remark, not with all these people here.'	'I can respond assertively to the remark Ray's just made by asking him what he means by it. I don't need to put him down in front of others.'
5. 'If I ask a question when I don't understand, I'll slow the meeting down and they may think I'm thick.'	'I can't contribute effectively if I don't understand. So I have the right to ask for clarification. It doesn't mean I'm thick.'
6. 'If I change my mind now I'll lose face and appear to be weak. I can't have that.'	'I can change my mind, if I want to. It can be a sign of strength rather than weakness.'

sound ones. Then you need to be clear about your rights as a member of a meeting, and to accept these rights.

Your rights as a member of a meeting

Most members are clear that the *chairman* of a meeting has certain rights: for example, the right to interrupt a member who is going on at great length. Also, members are usually fairly clear what these rights are, and they are prepared to give the chairman these rights in order for the meeting to progress. However, they are often less clear on their *own* rights as a member of a meeting. As with job rights in Chapter 3, we cannot be definitive about your rights in the meetings you attend. We can say, however, that the clearer you are on your rights, and the more you accept them, the more likely it is you will behave assertively in meetings. In the following we suggest some rights that you might have as a member of a meeting. You can then decide which ones you believe you have, or would like to have, and can work at accepting them. You may of course need to modify them in the light of your own experience.

We suggest you may have the right to:
- State your opinions and put forward suggestions
- Have these opinions and suggestions listened to and reacted to
- Understand what is being said
- Attend only those meetings, or parts of a meeting, that are relevant to you
- Spend your time productively in meetings
- Disagree with views and suggestions put forward by others
- Make your contributions without being interrupted by others
- Have minutes (where appropriate) that are an accurate reflection of what was said at the meeting
- Know in advance what the objective of the meeting is
- Know in advance roughly how long the meeting will last

As with all rights, accepting or failing to accept the above rights will affect your behaviour. For instance, if you do not accept the right about attending only meetings or parts of a meeting relevant to you, then you will find yourself sitting through all the items of an agenda when only two of them are relevant to you. While this is happening you are probably wanting to be getting on with some other work. Your earlier nonassertion will result in your now feeling restless and frustrated, until you start behaving aggressively, say, with a sarcastic comment about how long it takes the meeting to reach decisions. Accepting the right, on the other hand, encourages you to look for ways of attending just those parts relevant to you. Perhaps you can get the items on the agenda reordered so that you can leave the meeting when your items are over. This way you can reduce the amount of time you spend in meetings where you have nothing to contribute.

So having sound inner dialogues and accepting your rights moves you part way towards being more effective in meetings. In addition, there are certain *responsibilities* that go with your rights. In the next section we refer to these responsibilities at various times and also look at ways of behaving assertively in meetings *in line with* your rights and responsibilities.

Hints for contributing assertively to meetings

Many people believe that the responsibility for a meeting's effectiveness rests solely with the chairman. But we believe that *all members as well as the chairman have a responsibility to help the meeting to be effective.* Many of the following items develop from this responsibility.

MAKING YOUR CONTRIBUTIONS

So far in the book we have covered a number of aspects about behaving assertively that will also be relevant to meetings. Here, we highlight some ways of making your contributions so that they fit in with what we see as an important responsibility—that of *controlling* your own behaviour so that it helps rather than hinders the progress of the meeting.

Keep your contributions short
Your point is more likely to be understood and to have impact if you keep it reasonably short. The longer it is, the more difficult it is for others to understand and remember it. Your message becomes diluted. At the same time, the more you say, the more options you give others about which part of your contribution to respond to. Suppose you make the following statement:

'I've been thinking about this business of the workflow through the department. It seems to me that we've been having some bottlenecks in the invoice section. — *Diagnosis of problem*
So I think we could overcome these if we changed the system to having . . . — *Suggested solution*
Then we'd get a quicker response to . . . — *Benefit*
and at the same time we'd . . .' — *Benefit*

Let us assume that in the above example you want people to react to your suggestion. However, because you have put forward a suggestion as well as a statement of the problem and of the benefits, they are just as likely to react to any one of these three parts. Thus if someone disagrees, say, with one of your stated benefits, you are in danger of losing your suggestion altogether. Also, when people have several options about what parts to react to, the discussion often becomes fragmented.

So making no more than one or two points within any one contribution makes life easier for others, gives more impact to your contribution, and helps you control which parts people react to.

136

Avoid interrupting others to make your contribution, and do not let others interrupt you

When more people follow the first hint above, the whole business of interrupting is less of an issue. But in some meetings it is difficult to get in with your contribution, and once you are in, there is a temptation to make several of your points in one go, for fear of not getting in again! This sets up the vicious circle of others thinking you are going on a bit, and so giving themselves the right to interrupt you. Your fears are then confirmed; and so it goes on. There is no easy answer to this, but a starting point is to put your own house in order by keeping your contributions short. If you do this then you have the right to hold off interruptions by saying things like 'I'd just like to finish the point I'm making'. Having exercised your right not to be interrupted, it is important for you to accept the responsibility that goes with it: of not interrupting others. There may be exceptions to this when it is legitimate to interrupt, for instance when people are reducing the meeting's effectiveness with quite lengthy irrelevancies or repeats of previous points.

Keep your nonverbal behaviours assertive

Both the volume and the tone of voice are important here. If you speak too quietly your contribution will lose impact and be open to interruptions. It may not even be heard by some members! Especially if you shuffle papers at the same time or talk with your hand over your mouth.

In a meeting, eye contact takes on added significance. If you 'catch the chairman's eye' you can actually get in to make your contribution. Then, while you are making your contribution you want to distribute your eye contact between the chairman and the members for whom your contribution has most relevance. This enables you to judge how your contribution is being received by other people and in turn to signal to them that you are wanting a response.

TIMING YOUR CONTRIBUTIONS

If you want to influence a meeting, it is not just *what* you say that counts, but also *when* you say it.

If you fail to raise a point at the *relevant* time, then its impact is diminished. So if an item on the agenda has been dealt with, then it is unlikely that others will respond very positively to your reopening it, however 'good' your statement. If you are in a meeting where the boundaries between various items are not that clear-cut, then you may not be sure whether your point is relevant at that time. You can save the meeting a lot of time and confusion if you check this out with the chairman: 'Would it be relevant at this stage to make a point about . . .?'

Another timing trap you can fall into is *waiting until the last minute* before airing an opposite view. If other people are on the verge of making a decision when you suddenly come up for the first time with your doubts or disagreements, then other people will be irritated ('Why didn't you say that earlier?'). If people see you as having hesitated in raising your doubts (n.a.), then they may give little attention to them. But if they see you as having deliberately held back till the last minute (perhaps to create a more dramatic effect), then they may give attention to the doubts you raise, but at the same time they will probably feel somewhat resentful. This may show itself in aggressive behaviour towards you. So be assertive and do not hold back on your doubts and disagreements.

GETTING A REACTION TO YOUR CONTRIBUTION

If you follow the first two hints you stand a good chance of getting a reaction. If, however, after making your contribution, no one reacts to it, then we suggest you ask the meeting or a particular member for a reaction. You can say 'What do you all think about the suggestion I just made?' or 'Ron, do you agree with my point about . . .?' You do of course need to accept that you have a right to a reaction to a contribution, before you are likely to ask the above questions.

If one member disagrees, this may not necessarily represent the view of the rest of the meeting. It is assertive to ask others for their reactions. This way you get a picture of the whole meeting's reaction, rather than that of one or two individuals.

When people disagree with your contribution without giving a reason, we believe you have the right to ask for a reason. This will help you to see ways of modifying your own suggestion or of developing other people's suggestion, to overcome the objections raised.

We do not wish to give the impression here that you have the right to really push your ideas and force them upon others. The aim of getting a reaction is not necessarily to get your suggestions *accepted* (although it is nice if they are) but to have them *considered*. If you let others ignore your suggestions you are being nonassertive. If you try and force them on others, when it is clear they do not agree with them, then you are being aggressive.

If you accept the right to a reaction to your contributions, then you have the responsibility to react to the contributions that others make. This reaction can be in the form of agreeing, developing a suggestion (as explained in Chapter 11), or disagreeing. Disagreements need to be made assertively, for example in the form of 'I disagree with the suggestion because . . .'. Dismissive disagreements of the 'That'll never work' or 'That's not on' type are of course aggressive and have the effect of stifling ideas.

CHANGING YOUR MIND

It can be assertive to do this, especially in the light of new information or better ideas coming up in the meeting. Changing your mind assertively entails

138

your being honest and open about it and not apologizing. So you can say something like: 'In the light of what you said, Tom, I've changed my mind—I'm in favour of . . .'. If you stick defiantly with your original view because you don't want to be seen as weak or indecisive, then you are being aggressive.

FALLING IN WITH THE MAJORITY

We said earlier that, if you give yourself the right to make various contributions to a meeting, then you also have the responsibility to control your contributions so they help the meeting to progress. Because of this, it will sometimes be assertive to fall in with the majority. Suppose that, after making your views and ideas known, you find yourself in the minority. You then explore all the options but fail to come up with a way round the disagreement, and you realize time is pressing on. At this stage it would be assertive to fall in with the majority rather than prevent the meeting from progressing. We suggest you avoid an aggressive response like 'Well, have it your way, then' or a nonassertive response like 'Oh, all right' or 'I suppose so'. Better to let the meeting know how you stand: 'I don't see a way round the disagreement. I really prefer . . . but in view of the time, I'm happy to go along with the idea about . . .'

NOT FALLING IN WITH AN 'APPARENT' MAJORITY

Having heard a suggestion from a colleague, you may in your own mind disagree with it. If, however, two influential members of the meeting support the idea, you may be tempted to keep quiet about your disagreement or even to change your mind, saying to yourself 'Well, if they support it, it must be OK'. This nonassertion may result in a valid point about the feasibility of the suggestion being lost. Worse still, it may lead to a snowball effect in that other members keep quiet about their doubts. This way suggestions with only minimal support get accepted by the meeting. To prevent this domination of a meeting by a small number of people (who *appear* to be a majority) you need to accept that you have a responsibility to make your doubts and disagreements known.

DECIDING WHICH ISSUES TO BE ASSERTIVE ON

If in a particular meeting you find yourself out of line with the majority of views being expressed, there will be many issues on which you could take an assertive stand. There is a danger that, if you take a stand on *every* such issue, it will become counter-productive. Other members will start labelling you in their own minds as 'awkward' or 'negative'. This will colour their opinion of your views, and so any valid points you make will be lost.

The key is to decide the crucial issues on which you want to stand firm, or speak out. Restricting yourself in this way makes it more likely that your views on these issues will be taken into account.

HELPING THE MEETING TO IMPROVE ITS EFFECTIVENESS

If you give yourself the right to spend your time productively in meetings, then you will take on a degree of responsibility for the way the meeting is organized. This will lead you to put forward suggestions for how a meeting might improve its effectiveness by making changes in its approach. This is in contrast to the fairly common view that sees suggestions in this area as the prerogative of the chairman. So if he does not organize the meeting very well, then that is hard luck for you as a member but there is nothing you can do, but curse under your breath!

But if, on the other hand, you accept the above responsibility, then it is assertive to put forward suggestions about such things as:

– Setting a finishing time for the whole meeting or for the different items on the agenda
– Using flip charts or blackboards to capture ideas
– Having five minutes to study the pages of information you have just been presented with
– Tackling items in a different order or in a different way

When you make these suggestions you can avoid showing up the chairman if you use:

'I' statements: 'I would find it helpful if we took out five minutes to read the information.'

or

Responsive assertions: 'How about spending no more than half an hour on this one?'

Sometimes the meeting's effectiveness would be improved if you were to influence the *behaviour of other members*. Here are some examples of what we mean:

– Asking a member who has made a long 'speech' to summarize his main points
– Inviting a quiet member to contribute when you see he is trying (unsuccessfully) to get into the discussion
– Asking a member who is continually disagreeing what suggestion he has that he would like to see taken up by the meeting
– Asking the chairman for a summary, when you feel the meeting is getting bogged down
– Asking a colleague, whose nonverbal behaviours seem to indicate agreement or disagreement, to make his views known

These are examples of influencing people's behaviour *for the better*—to be more helpful to the meeting. Again, this is an area that is traditionally seen as the chairman's preserve. When he is not handling this side of things very well, we believe you have got not just a right but also a responsibility to try and help the meeting along. It is crucial to be clearly assertive when you are doing this.

It is also crucial that you do not make too many contributions in this area; otherwise you will be seen as trying to take over the meeting! Once this happens, the quality of the content of your contributions will be overlooked and the 'suspected' motive behind your making them becomes the dominant issue to which others react.

Conclusion

Meetings can, we believe, benefit from increased assertiveness from members and chairmen. You can make a start on this process for yourself in the next meeting you attend. First of all, check that your inner dialogue is sound; then pick out two or three of the above hints that will be most useful to you initially, and concentrate on these.

If you were previously nonassertive in meetings then you may decide to exercise only certain of your rights and responsibilities to start with. For instance, you might start with short, low-risk contributions like making your agreement more explicit, or asking for clarification. Once you have started the process of making more contributions, then you will feel more confident later on to exercise other rights and responsibilities.

If you were previously aggressive in meetings, you could make a start at being more assertive, say, by making your disagreements assertively and by looking for ways of developing other people's suggestions.

13. Continuing to increase your assertiveness

As we have gone along in this book, we have suggested that you take time out from reading to practise some of the things we are talking about. In this last chapter we aim to help you keep your learning going, so that you continue to become more assertive.

As we have said before, although it is not easy, you can change your behaviour if you want to. Your life to date has consisted of a continual process of changing—acquiring various patterns of behaviour, and then adjusting some and discarding others. But so far this process has not always been under your conscious control, so some of the behaviours were acquired in a random way. Because of this it is likely you have some behaviours that in retrospect you now consider to be less productive and rewarding than other behaviours. So the issue is not about whether you can or cannot change, but rather about whether you take control of those changes or not. The point is that you can direct the changes in whatever way you want them to go.

We will assume that you want to change your behaviour in the direction of increasing your assertion! So what can you do to make sure your efforts will lead to increased assertion as opposed to increased aggression or nonassertion? We would like to highlight the following four steps:
– Choosing the right situations
– Preparing for these situations
– Behaving assertively during these situations
– Reviewing situations afterwards
We will give some hints on each of these steps in turn.

Choosing the 'right' situations

Changes in behaviour come in small steps. So choose situations in which you believe *you have a reasonably good chance of maintaining your assertion, and of achieving a mutually acceptable outcome*. If you choose very difficult situations initially (for instance, standing up to a very aggressive senior manager), then you may be trying to take too big a step. Failure at this stage may lead you into having a faulty dialogue ('I knew it wouldn't work when it came to the crunch') and also to reducing your confidence in your ability to implement what you have learned.

Other factors to consider in selecting situations are *the benefits and consequences* that can follow from your increased assertion in a situation. This is particularly important when you are moving from nonassertion to

142

assertion. So you need to weigh the benefits against the possible negative consequences of standing up for your rights. Ideally, you are looking for situations where the benefits clearly outweigh any negative consequences. Making requests or giving praise are good examples of this.

Preparing for situations

This is crucial, in our experience. If you can spend a short while before an important situation working through the following steps, then you are more likely to be successful in that situation:
– Getting clear what you want to achieve from the situation (your objective)
– Clarifying your and the other person's rights
– Turning any faulty dialogues into sound ones
– Playing out in your own mind the assertive statements with which you want
  to start the interaction
Initially, you may want to jot down some notes under each of these headings. Later on you can dispense with notes and just get things clear in your own mind. You can do this as you travel to work or even in the two or three minutes as you walk to the office of the other person involved. You can practise saying to yourself the actual words you will use, along with the appropriate tone of voice. This will help you to start off the interaction on an assertive note. If you start off badly on an aggressive or nonassertive note, it can be difficult to recover.

Also, it can be helpful to work out your responses to some of the predicted 'hassles' that the other person may make. By 'hassles' we mean the statements that people use when they do not accept your assertion. Tables 13.1 and 13.2, which are examples of preparation for situations, include some instances of hassles. We are not necessarily suggesting that you go into this much detail in preparing; we have done so simply to illustrate the approach. Also, we have added a description of the situations to put the examples into context.

Behaving assertively during these situations

Having done some preparation along the lines described, you have a *healthy* degree of confidence in the situation itself. With this sort of confidence you are more likely to behave assertively. If you make your initial assertion as planned, this should get you off to a good start. If the predicted hassles come up, you can also handle them as planned.

It is possible that unexpected hassles will come up. The key to handling these is to 'buy yourself some time' in order to get a sound inner dialogue going and to think of an assertive response. You can do this very quickly. When we talk of buying time we are thinking of split seconds or seconds at the most. Here are some ways of 'buying time':

143

Table 13.1. Preparation for situations: Example 1

Description of situation
A request for capital expenditure. My manager (Ian) has agreed it, and it now needs to be approved by his manager (Ron). Ron has a lot of other expenditure requests and he is very busy at present. I am due to see him later today, with Ian, to make my case. Ian tends to become nonassertive in this sort of situation.

My objective in this situation
To get Ron to approve my capital expenditure request

Rights in situation

(a) Mine:	I believe I have the right to:
	– Put my case for the request and have it listened to
	– Expect Ian to make it clear that he is in favour of it
(b) Other person:	I believe Ron has the right to:
	– A clear presentation of the facts, both for and against
	– Make the final decision

Inner dialogue

Faulty dialogue	*Equivalent sound dialogue*
'Ron has so many other requests. He's so busy I can't see how I stand a chance of convincing him.'	'My request is as important as anyone else's, and I believe I can make out a good case for it.'
'Ian will do his usual trick of keeping his head down and won't support me.'	'It would be nice to have Ian actively supporting me, but if not I can get Ron's agreement on my own.'

My initial assertion
'Ron, about this capital expenditure request of mine: I appreciate that you have a lot of others to deal with. However, I believe there are substantial benefits that will follow from this expenditure.'

Predicted hassles	*Assertive responses*
'They'll need to be substantial; things are really tight at the moment.'	'I do see the benefits as substantial and would like to outline them to you.'
'It sounds all right, but how can you be sure you'll make those savings?'	'The savings I've mentioned are based on a detailed comparison that I've made with last year's figures. I believe they are realistic.'

144

Table 13.2. Preparation for situations: Example 2

Description of situation
Mike, one of my staff, is being considered for promotion to section manager. This is a newly created position within my department. He has recently been involved in a couple of tricky situations, which my director (Doug) believes he did not handle very well. Mike has a good record of success over the two years he has been with me, and I believe he should be offered the section manager's job.

My objective in this situation
To get Doug's agreement to offer Mike the section manager's job

Rights in situation
(a) Mine: I have the right to make up my own mind about Mike and to recommend him for the job.
(b) Other person: Doug has the right to make the final decision on whether Mike is offered the job.

Inner dialogue

Faulty dialogue	*Equivalent sound dialogue*
'I know Doug doesn't rate Mike, so if I disagree with his judgement, he'll doubt my judgement.'	'Just because my judgement is different from Doug's doesn't mean it's wrong.'
'Doug's biased, and nothing I can say will make him change his mind.'	'I think that Doug has formed his opinion of Mike on the basis of recent events. I can give him evidence of Mike's good work over the past two years. He may change his mind after this.'

My initial assertion
'Doug, before you finally make up your mind about Mike, I'd like to discuss his overall performance with you.'

Predicted hassles	*Assertive responses*
'I think the last couple of weeks have convinced me that he's not the man for the job.'	'I recognize that Mike did not handle those recent situations well, but I think they were very tricky ones. I'd like to put that alongside his good performance over the past two years.'
'I don't think Mike has the stuff that managers are made of.'	'Well, can we identify the areas that you think Mike is weak in?'

145

– Weighing of words: 'Well, . . .' 'Fine, . . .' 'OK, . . .' 'I see, . . .'
– Responsive assertions, in the form of seeking clarification or testing your understanding: 'Do you mean . . .?' or 'Have I got it right, what you're saying is . . .?'
– Asking for 'time out': 'I'd like a moment to think about that', or 'Let me see now', or 'Now, let me ponder this'.

Reviewing situations afterwards

As you walk back to your office or travel home in the evening, you will probably find yourself thinking about the situations you have been involved in. When you are doing this, it is essential to be realistic about both your successes and your failures.

When you are considering your successes, do not down-play them, or exaggerate them. Being honest with yourself about your successes provides you with an objective basis for making progress in the future.

Because you are trying out new or modified approaches in handling situations, you may be unsuccessful in any of the following ways:
– You fail to maintain your assertion
– You do not achieve your objective
– The other person does not accept your right to be assertive
In all these cases you want a sound inner dialogue afterwards, so that you can rationally analyse what happened and learn from it. Faulty dialogues like 'I knew I'd mess it up' will work against your learning from the situation. In contrast, sound dialogues like the following ones help to ensure that you keep on developing your assertive skills:
– 'I wasn't successful in achieving my objective, but I reckon I know why.'
– 'Roy responded aggressively, and I think found it difficult to accept that I have the right to suggest alternative approaches. I can clarify this with him next time it happens.'
As a result of reviewing your behaviour in this way, you can work out improved responses to the situations that you can predict will occur. You can also start working on other areas of your assertiveness in which you feel you can make improvements. At the same time, you can begin to increase your assertion in some of those more difficult situations that we suggested you avoid tackling early on. So, having got some successes under your belt, you can choose, for instance, to stand up to the very aggressive senior manager that we referred to early on in this chapter. However, before rushing into action on this, we suggest you consider the benefits and consequences and prepare carefully, so that you are clear beforehand on how far you are going to push your assertion.

Handling unexpected situations

Sometimes, of course, you are not able to prepare for situations—for instance, when someone bursts into your office and is aggressive to you about a new policy announcement. It usually helps in such situations if you buy yourself some time in the way we described earlier in this chapter.

In the early days of learning to be more assertive, these situations can be very demanding. It is important, therefore, to be realistic about your performance in these situations. Do not berate yourself afterwards with such statements as: 'Why didn't I think of it at the time? What I should have said to him was . . .'

A final few words

A lasting increase in your assertion will come about only if you do keep practising and reviewing. This way, the assertive behaviours we have referred to in the book become an integrated part of your behaviour. Being realistic when you review your performance ensures that you recognize your successes and keep your failures in perspective. It may help you to understand some of these failures if you remember that some people may have a vested interest in your *not* becoming more assertive.

Index

Aggression:
    definition, 2
    different levels of, 102–103
    effects of, 9–13
    how it comes about, 13–15
    nonverbal aspects of, 32–33
    recognition exercise, 26–29
    source of, 19
    verbal aspects of, 23
Aggression from others:
    barriers to assertive responses, 103–105
    faulty inner dialogues about, 104
    model for responding to, 105–113
Assertion:
    definition, 1
    nonverbal aspects of, 32–33
    recognition exercise, 26–29
    verbal aspects of, 21
    why use more, 15–18

Basic assertion, 56–57
Belief system, 36–37
Beliefs:
    about disagreeing, 50–51
    about giving praise, 52
    about making requests, 45–46
    about receiving praise, 54
    about refusing requests, 47
Buying time, 143, 146

Complementary needs, 124
Conflict:
    guidelines for resolving, 128–132
    ways of handling, 125–128
Conflicting needs, 125
Consequence assertion, 60

Decision making:
    faulty dialogues about, 100
    influencing your, 95–100
Disagreeing:
    aggressively, 50
    assertively, hints for, 51

beliefs about, 50–51
    nonassertively, 51
Discrepancy assertion, 58–59

Empathetic assertion, 57–58

Feelings:
    productive, 70
    unproductive, 70, 73, 78
    ways of handling, 70–71
    where they come from, 71–73

Giving criticism:
    common inner dialogues, 86
    guidelines, 86–91
    rights involved, 86
Giving praise:
    beliefs about, 52
    hints for, 53

Hassles, 143

Influence:
    through aggression, 95–97
    through assertion, 98
    through nonassertion, 97–98
    through past behaviour, 99–100
    two elements of, 94–95
Inner dialogues:
    about giving criticism, 86
    about meetings, 134–135
    about other's aggression, 104
    about receiving criticism, 92
    intervening with, 78–84

Making requests:
    beliefs about, 45
    hints for making, 46–47
    rights involved, 46
Meetings:
    hints for contributing to, 136–141
    inner dialogues about, 134–135
    responsibilities of members, 136
    rights of members, 135

Needs:
    accepting, 130
    identifying, 128
    types of, 124–125
Negative feelings assertion, 59–60
Nonassertion:
    definition, 1
    different forms, 117–120
    effects of, 3–6
    how it comes about, 6–9
    nonverbal aspects of, 32–33
    recognition exercise, 26–29
    source of, 19
    verbal aspects of, 22
Nonassertion from others, responding
    assertively to, 120–123
Nonimpacting needs, 124
Nonverbal behaviour, associated with
    assertion, nonassertion, aggres-
    sion, 32–33

Persistence, 49
Preparing for situations, examples,
    144–145
Put-downs, 113–115

Receiving criticism:
    hints for, 92–93
    inner dialogues, 92
    rights involved, 92
Receiving praise:
    beliefs about, 54
    hints for, 54
Refusing requests:
    beliefs about, 47
    hints for, 48
Responsibilities, 42

Responsive assertion, 60–61
Rights:
    acceptance of, 39
    definition, 3
    general rights, 36–40
    in giving criticism, 86
    in meetings, 135
    in receiving criticism, 92
    job rights, 40–42
    other people's, 43
    why important, 35

Sarcasm, 32, 53
Self-esteem, 19
Stating views (see Disagreeing)

Thinking process:
    faulty, 76
    nature of, 74
    sound, 76
Types of assertion:
    basic, 56–57
    consequence, 60
    discrepancy, 58–59
    empathetic, 57–58
    exercise, 67–69
    how to say, 63–65
    negative feelings, 59–60
    responsive, 60–61
    summary table, 66–67
    when to use, 62–63

Verbal aspects of behaviour:
    of aggression, 23
    of assertion, 21
    of nonassertion, 22
    summary table, 25